P9-BZO-821

ALL IN THE NAME OF THE LORD

By Bill Stringfellow

Love —
To the Kujawas
from Bill +
Sharon
2-2-87

CONCERNED PUBLICATIONS, INC.
"Publishers With A Purpose"
Clermont, Florida

Concerned Publications
Box 1024,
Clermont, Florida 32711

Copyright © 1980 by William W. Stringfellow, Jr.

Library of Congress Catalog Card Number: 49-329

ISBN 0-939286-00-9

Fifth Printing, 1984

Printed in the United States of America

CONTENTS

1/THE SCHEME

Charles Dawson found them in a gravel pit in Piltdown Common in Sussex, England in 1912. The scientific world became ecstatic! Now the "missing link" between the ape and man has been discovered! Charles Darwin's theory of evolution is now a fact!

Kenneth Oakley had some doubts. The geologist submitted the bones to a special chemical analysis. He announced that he had some serious doubts about the bones that were supposed to be those of an animal-human in between the ape and man.

Then, in 1953, new and complicated tests were made and the truth was known. The "missing link" proved to be the jawbone of the longarmed orangutan ape whose teeth had been ingeniously filed and stained in a special heat process to appear very old.

A harmless hoax? The British Museum doesn't think so. You see, not only did they first authenicate the bones as the genuinely long-sought-after "missing link" but honored Dawson by naming the bones "Eoanthropus Dawsoni" after his name.

It was just a simple swindle, but, something happened to you when you read those words that you probably are not even aware of. It was a very minute happening but, nevertheless, it happened to you. Psychiatrists and psychologists tell us that every time we read or hear about something depressing or discouraging both our emotions and our physical condition is affected and not for the best.

What happened to you when you learned of the recent disclosure that an American corporation, one of the largest, did not pay any taxes in 1974 and 1975? Not only did that company take advantage of foreign and investment tax credits to keep from paying one red cent of income tax, but actually a refund over those two years was given to it that reached an amount well over 189,000,000 dollars!

How were you affected when you learned that that firm was one of the auto industry's "big three"? That psychological and physiological let down took place even while you just read it now.

The well-dressed and personable man from the Federal Reserve Bank was investigating questionable acts in some lending institutions across America. He was simply substantiating accounts by personally contacting savers at random. When pushed by the senior citizens on whom he was making this particular call, he admitted that there were some irregularities in the savings and loan association where they were depositors. When pressed even further he suggested, without telling anyone else and starting a run on the bank, that they withdraw their savings. He suggested a "safer" bank. He would help if they did not disclose it. He was very kind. He had all the forms in his briefcase. Hard-earned savings accumulated over twenty-five years were withdrawn from the "questionable" savings and loan association to be deposited in a dependable one. That concerned public servant had helped the aged couple prevent a tragic loss. He even went to the lending institution himself to make the transfer. But, the money, once withdrawn, was never re-deposited. He kept it and disappeared! The retired couple, like reported thousands of others, lost every dime they had saved.

How does it feel to be defrauded?

What would you think if you were being swindled in one of the most sinister schemes ever conceived? Millions are.

Disappointment? You know what it means.

You experience some of it when you put several coins in the machine to get a cold drink and it comes out warm. A cold pizza not only irritates you, it continues to set up a chain of mental depressions already in process through other disappointments in times past.

The new car dealer "just can't find anything wrong" with your car. The "lemon" automobile makes you sour!

Even one cracked egg in a carton of twelve makes you wonder if you will get value for your money again.

The candy bars get smaller and smaller. Yet, the prices do not decrease with the size but actually increase. That bothers you!

Then there was the "Watergate" scandal! You might not have voted for Richard Nixon, and you might not have thought the bugging of opponent politicians was such a serious offense, but the way it was all covered up and the American people lied to, really hurt you. It just opened another empty spot in your already punctured confidence in governmental leaders and politicians. Another disappointment!

Ralph Nader. Just the mention of his name and immediately millions fear an announcement of another trusted and much-used product being hazardous to their health. How can some pharmaceutical and drug companies fleece the elderly and sick with so-called miracle drugs that have no meaningful and helpful ingredients? Even the ill are deceived. That really did it!

Nearly 1,000 men, women, and young people are all dead, senselessly dead! Duped by a deceiver. Those mass-murders and suicides in sun-drenched Guyana added a great deal to the chain of mental depression and distrust. Whom can you trust?

Jim Jones was not the first nor the last. Hardly a week goes by but some new scandal comes to light. More and more religious personalities are exposed because of double standards. Many well-heeled church leaders who are simply trying to "do good" unto others are doing quite well! This really hurts!

3

All of us want to see one institution, one organization be above all the deception, fraud, dishonesty, misrepresentation, embezzlement, indecency, and political maneuvering that is par for the course for twentieth century America. In spite of all the criticism it is receiving today, we want that one establishment to stand head and shoulders above it all, and that is the church! We want to look up to that one highly-respected place of worship again. We all want it to remain the epitome of everything good and wholesome. We want it to be the untouched center of our society and the perfect representation of truth, righteousness, and justice.

It disturbs us to read about a certain church giving "S & H Green Stamps" to its attendants in return for their offerings.

We want to erase all these things forever from our minds and be able to turn to that one institution and point to it with pride. So, when the story leaks out about another minister, evangelist, priest, rabbi, and church leader slipping his hand into the till, carrying on an affair, or deluding sincere seekers of the truth, we try to pretend we never heard it. Ignore the rumors and they will go away. But, with all your efforts to ignore it, that chain reaction of distrust and depression continues to increase and work a deadly work.

You are about to discover a world-wide hoax that is defrauding millions, maybe even you. You are going to launch into the reading of a diabolical scheme that seems almost impossible to conceive much less carry out with astonishing success! This deception deals with that one place in life you never, ever wanted to see touched—the church! You see, this stunning swindle of all swindles has been perpetrated "All in the Name of the Lord."

Now you are starting to say to yourself, "Man, I'm not being deceived. I know what I believe and why. I'm pretty solid. I'm sound and no self-ordained messiah is going to ever brainwash me. I surely can see through guys like Jim Jones, Sun Myung Moon, David "Moses" Berg, Guru Maharaj Ji, Swami Prahhupada, and Paul Erdman. I may not go to church like some avid members do, but I'll never be swept away by some religious fad. I'm not being swindled, that's for sure." Well, wait a minute! What would happen if you found out that what you have been accepting as fact actually turned out to be more like fiction? Impossible? Well, what would happen if, by the strangest happenings, those tangibles turned out to be intangible under careful investigation? Can you handle it if some new discovery proved that those canons you have so confidently considered conventional were not correct after all? ——

What if, by the stretching of your imagination, you were confronted with new illumination that indicated that your norms proved to be abnormal? Even though it seems absolutely impossible at this time and place, how would you react to the knowledge that your ideologies were incorrect and illogical? Can you honestly state that your concepts can stand a complete challenge?

Maybe this con job, which happens to be the most concentrated one since planet earth's creation, will only prove you have been correct after all.

Maybe this swindle, which happens to be the most sensational and successful one since man's first breath, will only make you appreciate your being even more solid in your beliefs than you ever believed. Maybe your understanding this fraud, which happens to be the most fantastic one you will ever try to fathom, will only make you deeply thankful that somehow you never fell under its hypnotic control.

Maybe.

Protestants, Jews and Catholics alike agree in the belief that there is a Supreme Being who created our planet, solar system, and us. That Supreme Being is God. God is sinless and holy. He communicated with His created beings on earth in person, but being sinless, God could not personally communicate with these created beings once they had sinned. A barrier came between God and man. That led to the written communication—the Bible. A message from the Master to man, from the Creator to the

5

beings He had created. It is a book of regulations and instructions for humanity's advancement and happiness.

All right, think about this. One God. One book from God for man. Why, then, are there so many "gods", religions, and so-called "divine writings?"

Why Protestantism, Catholicism, and Judiasm in modern, advanced America? Why several divisions within Catholicism and Judiasm? Why are there over 250 different denominations within Protestantism alone, all from one basic textbook?

Go further. The "American Religious Big Three" (Protestantism, Catholicism, and Judiasm) teach that without a shadow of a doubt the Supreme Being who created us loves us in a far more meaningful relationship than the finest human father of his children. God cares about His creations. He acts in behalf of their happiness and security. So, then, how can there be any such thing as war, disease, pain, and death?

Go even further. A sinless, pure, holy, and loving God created human beings in His image. He made them sort of miniatures or duplications. How, then, could a sinless, pure, holy and loving image, miniature or duplication ever conceive an impure thought, a sinful act, an expression of hate or an unholy life?

This Supreme Being, God, is the Author and Originator of order, perfection, holiness and sinlessness.

That one loving God made one code of ethics in one communique for His creatures, the Bible. It is the secret for success, the prescription for happiness. How could anyone ask for more?

But . . . what went wrong?

How did it all fail?

Where did such a perfect system bog down?

Who threw in the monkey wrench?

Remember the story? Adam and Eve, the first human beings on planet earth, were made free moral agents. Higher order than animals, they had the power of choice. One restriction was placed over the perfect pair's life in perfect paradise. There was one test of obedience, love, and faith in their Creator. One tree was off limits. The fruit of that tree was not to be eaten. Eve drifted from her husband one day and made her way to that forbidden tree. In the tree was a beautiful serpent who had the ability to also communicate with humans. Dazzling in beauty and charm, the serpent tricked the woman into eating the fruit. Eve persuaded her mate to eat of it too, and the rest is all history. "Sin" became a tragic shadow over earth.

Now, please consider these vital questions. How was it that there was an evil power, a demon, a beguiling spirit, in the midst of a perfect paradise placed on this planet by a perfect God? Did he somehow slip by an all-seeing God? How did a highly intelligent being possess a beautiful serpent's body and speak through it to present a temptation that could lead to such eternally destructive consequences?

Two little boys attended church one day. Walking home together afterwards both were unusually quiet. One, turning to the other, said, "I sure did get kinda scared when the preacher was talking about the Devil, didn't you?"

"Yea," the other lad replied, "But I'm not now."

"Yea, how come?"

"Well, I've been thinking about it and I've figured it all out."

"You have? Whatta you mean?"

"Well," the lad replied in a serious and sober manner, "It's just like the Santa Claus story. The Devil will turn out to be your daddy."

Is the Devil a fact or fiction? The success of the comedian Flip Wilson was enhanced by his much-repeated excuse for wrong-doing, "The Devil made me do it." The Bible writers discuss this being many times in many ways. The ministry today blames him for all our problems. Little children are taught that he is God's enemy and theirs too.

Many Christians believe that the Devil was an angel. Common sense tells you that if any one thing exists, or existed, it had to have a beginning, an origin. Theologians and Bible scholars have started to come to the understanding of questions puzzling sincere people for centuries. Along with the sudden advancement and achievements by scientists, chemists, and medical researchers, the ones concerned with spiritual matters are, too, acquiring new knowledge and insight. No longer do these men of the cloth demonstratively portray a forked, tailed demon with split hoofs of tradition.

Just as it makes sense that planets cannot orbit in precise split-second accuracy and consistency, flowers cannot bloom with minutely intricate superstructures identical to the next flower of the same kind, the sun, moon, and stars cannot make their never-failing appearances in dependably accurate clock-like fashion, and man cannot be born with his millions of complex mechanisms without the origin and supervision of some Infinitely Intelligent Being. So cannot the havoc, disease, crime, injustice, and ultimate death so prevalent today operate without some infinitely degenerate being.

That being is revealed in the Bible as Lucifer or Satan. He is portrayed as more than just a symbol of everything opposite of good and lovely. So, then, how did he come into being, and come to be so degenerate?

Who made the Devil?

What is he really like? Does anyone know?

In the New Testament four men, recorded accurate accounts of Christ's words and actions. Since it would have taken five books, each as large as the entire Bible, to record all of His sayings and works, they relayed to us the major and vital ones. Those four books are called the "gospels." "Gospel" means "good news." They tried to preserve the "good news" of His life, death, burial, resurrection, and ascension. Those four gospel books are known simply by the authors. That is, Matthew, Mark, Luke and John.

In the gospel account of John, Jesus agreed with the fact that everything must have a beginning or origin. In the eighth chapter of John Christ makes it clear that the Devil not only had an origin, but he originated something himself. In verse 44, Christ said, "When he (the Devil) speaketh a

8

lie, he speaketh of his own; for he is a liar, and the father of it."

Throughout the four gospel books it is clearly seen that Jesus Christ accepted the fact that the Devil is a literal being. To Him Satan is no fantasy or fairytale. All of the New Testament, and Old Testament also, portrays this same concept. Satan is portrayed as an arch-enemy of God and mankind. But, where did this enemy get his start? Was it Heaven?

The Bible's description of Heaven, the center of the universe, is far more fascinating than most people realize. But, in a nonsuperstitious, sensible, and sane manner the Bible states that Heaven is the headquarters and homebase of the Creator. It is a literal, tangible, and visible place. It epitomizes everything that stands for beauty, honesty, fairness, love, and happiness. But, there is more!

According to both the Old and New Testaments Heaven is also the very place that the Devil came into being! You just cannot put Heaven and Satan in the same place, can you? But, get this: Heaven is where the Devil actually originated! Saint Luke's gospel account is a shocker to many when they discover chapter 10 and verse 18, which records the words of Jesus. They go like this: "I beheld Satan as lightning fall from heaven." Since everyone agrees that in order for someone to fall "from" a certain place, that someone would have had to "have been in" that place in the beginning, it appears that Satan was, at one time, in Heaven itself!

Was he a visitor or resident?

Isaiah was the Old Testament Prophet who told of the virgin birth of Christ centuries before. He also spoke a great deal about the crucifixion. He devoted many pages of his book to Heaven. But, not only did Isaiah confirm Christ's shocking statement about Satan having been in Heaven, he also gives us a detailed description of that arch-enemy. You might be amazed at what Isaiah said. In chapter 14 and verse 12, he records the Creator's words to Satan: "How art thou fallen, O Lucifer, son of the morning!

How art thou cut down to the ground, which didst weaken the nations." (more description later)

Protestants, Catholics, and Jews all agree that in these words are the pillars for the belief that this demon was removed from the headquarters of the Creator and was restricted to the limitations of earth. Added to all this is an elaboration by John in his prophetic book, Revelation. In the last book of the Bible there is the statement that the Devil was not alone when he was deported from Heaven. In Revelation 12:9, John says, "And the great dragon was cast out, that old serpent, called the Devil and Satan, which deceiveth the whole world, he was cast out into the earth, and his angels were cast out with him." Since the Bible scholars teach that the Bible always confirms everything it teaches, looking in other writings about Satan really adds up to an amazing and interesting picture.

Hidden in the Old Testament book of Ezekiel is a real jewel! It is a clear and concise answer to many questions. God speaks to Ezekiel and tells him what to say to a sinister king. He is told to compare the king of Tyrus to Satan himself. In chapter 28 and verses 12–15, are these revealing words: "Thus saith the Lord God, Thou sealest up the sum, full of wisdom, and perfect in beauty. Thou hast been in Eden the garden of God; every precious stone was thy covering, the sardius, topaz, and the diamond, the beryl, the onyx, and the jasper, the sapphire, the emerald, and the carbuncle, and gold; the workmanship of thy tabrets and of thy pipes was prepared in thee in the day that thou wast created. Thou art the anointed cherub that covereth; and I have set thee so; thou wast upon the holy mountain of God; thou hast walked up and down in the midst of the stones of fire. Thou was perfect in thy ways from the day that thou wast created, till iniquity was found in thee."

Even though the King James Version of the Bible, from which this was taken, is written in the Old English manner, we can still piece these odd terms together and discover an amazing revelation. Re-read it and you will see some fantastic facts.

Satan was created by God.

Satan was one of the two super-privileged angels, or cherubs, who actually stood at the throne of God reaching out one of their wings to the other angel's wing to form a covering, a canopy, an arch, over God!

Satan was created by God and was very handsome.

Satan's actions and examples were perfect. Perfect, that is, until sin originated within him.

This mystery of self-created sin has blown the minds of the greatest of theologians through the centuries until just recently.

Sin originating in Heaven?

Sin originating in the mind of one of the executives of the eternal? The most honored angel, the angel who held unequaled power and glory among all the angels, the angel in continuous presence of the very Creator of all beings actually sinning? Sin originating in the angel who drank in the beams of brilliant beauty that enshrouds God? Sin originating in the one who held an exalted position in the vast, vast universe? How could it happen? How did it happen?

The same Ezekiel who gave us some very interesting information about Satan adds more insight to the almost unfathomable questions dealing with that enemy of human lives. In the seventeenth verse of that same chapter he adds this: "Thine heart was lifted up because of thy beauty, thou hast corrupted thy wisdom by reason of thy brightness." It seems that every time Satan, or Lucifer as he was originally called, passed the crystal lake and looked at himself he had a miniature worship service right then and there. Slowly he began to indulge in self-admiration, and, as it has been said, when you start looking more and more at yourself you soon cannot see anything, or anyone else. Lucifer grew to the place where he could not see anyone but himself . . . . not even God! Soon, his high position in the kingdom was not enough. He was bright, talented in numerous things, and very useful. He wanted the top position. He wanted to become God! Sound impossible? History records many humans who thought they were God. Satan thought he was qualified to be God.

Isaiah has recorded Lucifer's aspirations. His own words have been preserved. In chapter 14 and verses 13 and 14 Lucifer's self-admiration before a full-length mirror sounded like this: "I will exalt my throne above the stars (the angels) of God . . . I will be like the Most High." He wanted the top position. He wanted to be the leader, president, chairman of the board. Now, no one rises to the top without the resignation, or retirement, of the president. A resignation? Naturally the Creator would not, nor could not, retire nor resign. So, there had to be a dismissal. There could not be a dismissal without a cause. So, then, in one of the most spectacular and sinister schemes ever conceived in all the annals of history, Lucifer began his insidious and ingenius plot. The impeachment of the God of Heaven! He had to win the favor of the majority, if not all, of the angels. His mastermind manufactured the method. In the affections and allegiances of the vast host of angels God held supreme. To win that same power and following he must bring them to the realization, he said, that this Supreme Authority over them all had ulterior, selfish, motives for His expressions of love and freedom. They must see that God is driven by an egotistical drive that can only be satisfied by the submission of all these angels to His every wish. These higher orders of life must see that the laws God has placed before all His creation could, and would, apply to those in the worlds of space, but surely not to the angels! They were wiser, more beautiful and excelled in strength! Since they were holy beings how could they do anything that was wrong? They did not need laws. They were being subjected to a needless and senseless code of ethics. The very existence of these codes proved that God did not really trust them. If He had true confidence in them why would he make laws to govern them?

Lucifer determined that he could overthrow the throne

12

of God if he could get the angels to believe that they were being held back in their growth and development. If these laws were repealed, along with the One who had made them, then these angels would enjoy a greater freedom and happiness, he began to quietly suggest. Lucifer began his insidious work behind the scenes. One by one, small groups here and there, he cunningly twisted the truth to make God appear as a tyrant, and, of course, himself a deliverer!

Being the Supreme God, and infinite in wisdom, the Lord watched lovingly and patiently as Lucifer worked his scandalous propaganda. Finally the time came for justice and mercy to step in.

God's spirit went out through the entire company of trusted angels, drawing them back to His love. Not everyone was fooled by the deceptive words of this covetous creature, but many were. The conflict intensified. Finally a decision must be made by all. Either they were to continue in their trust and confidence in the Creator, or adopt the teachings, and accept the charges of Lucifer. The book of Revelation reveals that, tragically, one-third of all these hosts of Heaven's angels fell for Lucifer's lies! In spite of the fact that the loyal angels pleaded with their deceived companions, and expressed their concern for the ultimate fate of disloyalty, the gap enlarged. Something had to happen.

Think about it for a moment. If you were the Supreme Head of the universe, what would you do? Would you drag this impostor in before the eyes of everyone and make an example out of him? Would you call a court session and let a jury decide? Lucifer was actually placing God in a position where he could use methods and tactics God could not. Lucifer could stretch the truth, color the picture, and deceive sincere minds. God could not and would not.

How do you defend yourself against false charges? Just as in our modern judicial system a man is innocent until proven guilty, the Creator threw the burden of proof back on Lucifer. It was Lucifer's responsibility to prove his charges. God could not allow Lucifer to remain in Heaven

13

no more than He could later allow fallen man to be in His Holy presence. So, then, Lucifer was shipped out to another area.

Lucifer eventually found one specific planet for his angels and himself. That planet . . . earth! Earth became the place where Lucifer was to prove his charges were true, not only to the angels in Heaven but to all the inhabitants of all the unfallen worlds of God's creation. After all, they would have questions about it, too.

Did you know that earth was the battleground? The apostle Paul knew it. In his first book to the Christians in Corinth he said that this earth had become that very special arena. In First Corinthians 4:9, he said that this earth and all its inhabitants are a "spectacle unto the world, and to angels, and to men."

"Spectacle." It is fantastic because that explosive word in the original language Paul wrote in, Greek, means "theatre." This was what inspired Shakespeare to write those famous words about all the world being a stage and the men and women actors. Imagine the world being a stage with the universe looking on!

It has only been in recent times that leading religionists have arrived at the understanding of why the Bible speaks several times about Satan being cast out of Heaven to earth. A stage where he tries to portray, through you and me, that he is correct in all his charges against God. Every accepted temptation, and every fall into sin, is a time for Satan to rejoice off stage. He took over planet earth when he caused the first actors to play his lines. When he tricked Adam and Eve into doubting God, Eve more than Adam by the way, it was just a duplication of what he had accomplished with one-third of the angels in Heaven. And now he stands off the wings of the stage, smirking smuggly, looking occasionally up into Heaven, shaking his fist at the throne of God, shouting at everyone there around God to look at the scenes being played out on the stage of life. "Look at how many follow my liberated way of life, and how few, if any at all, who are still following those old

14

restricting laws of yours." And he doesn't have to lie, does he? The actors are amazingly playing out his roles with artistic accuracy. He has the majority following him, doesn't he?

Why doesn't God step in, close the curtain, and ring down the last act of war, strife, sickness, poverty, death, divorce, broken homes, rape, murder, crooked politics, and false religions? Has it all gone beyond a point of no return?

Through the years ministers, priests and rabbis have repeated one theme over and over again. That theme is summed up in the words "God is Love." It is simple. "God is Love." Yet, so sublime and raftering above the heights of our comprehension! Many defeated and dejected souls have been turned away from religion because of the inability of some to answer the question, "How can a God of love let these things happen?" Are God's hands tied? Will the play of life continue to be a sell-out and play forever? Why doesn't God bring it all to an end? Why did He allow the curtain to roll open in the first place? It has only played terrible scenes. Look at a much-repeated illustration and you've got the answer.

A young mother stares lovingly and appreciatively at that beautiful 18 inch-long little bundle in blue lying in her arms. It is so beautiful and is her very own child. Though so small it demands, and gets, such a large amount of love, care and attention. It is more precious than all the gold in all the world. It is her own child . . . harmless . . . her own child . . . helpless . . . her baby. She snuggles it to her breast. She takes it home from the hospital. Each feeding, diaper change, and special dressing for admiring visitors is another opportunity to love it. It is so very special to her. But, as time waits for no baby, it all too quickly grows into manhood and something happens! That sweet, loving and affectionate child, trained in correct morality, gets into the wrong crowd. A change takes place within him. He is drawn away from the decent and moral aspects of life into a life of crime. The mother's aching

15

heart pleads with him to no avail. Finally the son goes too far. He commits murder in the first degree. Then comes the soul-shaking, heart-rendering agony of the mother. Her son dies in the electric chair. Then, comes the indescribable shame. A long, long time passes before the mother is able to pull herself together again. A similarity to normality finally comes. It has been hard, but worth it. Then, one day, as she is in the laundramat, a neighbor walks over to her and begins a conversation. Eventually the talk gets around to the criminal son . . . the murderer. The neighbor shocks the mother with the question, "Well, why didn't you destroy that murderer when he was born?"

An innocent baby was born. Despite the loving care and instruction of the mother, he becomes a murderer. It was everything opposite from what the mother had planned for her child. Can the mother be held responsible? The man made a criminal and murderer out of himself. No one, in their right mind, would ever accuse a mother of bringing a murderer into the world, and no mother would ever kill her own son.

The epitome, the fullness, the extreme existence of love, God, the Creator, loved Lucifer His creation. God did not create a liar, a deceiver, a self-possessed demon. Lucifer made a devil out of himself. Like the murderer, Lucifer spurned all the wise counsel of his Loved One. Like the murderer, Lucifer, too, will one day ultimately pay for his crimes against God and mankind. But, the very existence of Satan is vivid proof of the existence and love of God. The creator cannot be blamed as a creator of evil.

A maddening pursuit of the overthrow of God! A great scheme. The methods, the modus operandi of Satan are almost impossible for the human mind to comprehend, but the definite pattern exists. The driving passion of Lucifer will be seen now as you embark on one of the most interesting and important researches of your life. The swindle of all swindles . . . fraud of all frauds . . . the hoax of all hoaxes.

2/COUNTERFEIT

The third grade. Class discussion. The subject . . . war! The teacher's questions were enthusiastically answered. Then came the stumper. "Does anyone know what a furlough is?"

No abundance of eager hands waving for recognition this time. Just one. It was Charlie's.

"It's a donkey," he replied without being recognized.

"A what?" the teacher asked.

"A donkey," Charlie replied with even more enthusiasm.

"Oh no, Charlie, a furlough is not a donkey. Where did you get such an idea as that?"

"Well, I know that it is a donkey," he pressed the point, "Because I have a picture of one at home. I can bring it tomorrow."

The teacher agreed, trying to warn him of his error to soften the blow of embarrassment. But, when school was over Charlie reminded the teacher that he was definitely going to bring the picture the next day.

The next day Charlie came into class carrying a large picture wrapped in brown paper. Time would not go fast enough before he could really prove to the class and the teacher that a donkey and a furlough were one and the same thing. He finally got to unwrap the paper and hold the picture up for everyone to see. It portrayed a picture of a soldier riding on a donkey.

17

"Look here," Charlie said, "It says, 'Father coming home on his furlough'." Seeing is believing? Too many times too many people share Charlie's mistake. That is, what is gleaned from certain words and sentences may not be the intended message after all. It may be just the opposite. How many times have you heard someone say, "Oh, you can make the Bible read any way you want to?" Too many times too many people miss the real importance and significance of a Biblical statement because of previous teachings and understandings. Far too many hidden "gems" are actually overlooked and ignored.

One such hidden "gem" of explosive Bible truth has been passed over and over again by the greatest majority of readers ever since the King James translation came rolling off the press. When understood as the Creator intended, it opens up an entirely new perspective. It is the hidden history that explains a lot of unanswered questions. You are going to be amazed at yourself for not seeing it sooner.

A simple historical account? Early man's family tree? At first it does seem so. For centuries it has been accepted as such, but, now the truth is finally being seen. What has been generally thought to be simply a list of the offsprings of Noah is actually the foundation for false faiths. It is the explanation as to how Satan began his shrewd start of counterfeiting Christianity. It is the ingenius method whereby millions and millions have been deceived and deluded. And as the pieces start to come together like a jig-saw puzzle, you will not only see it so very clearly, but you will be forced to do some self-examinations.

The first book in the Bible is called Genesis. It comes from the Latin and Greek word that means creation or beginning. In the tenth chapter of Genesis we have the list of Noah's descendants. Noah, you will remember, was the one who made the voyage across the flooded world in a durable and serviceable ark. After the excursion trip in the gigantic ocean vessel, Noah and his wife took their three sons and daughters-in-law and started to rebuild a new world. Beginning with the first verse, the expansion of those families is recorded. It goes like this: "Now these are the generations of the sons of Noah, Shem, Ham and Japheth: and unto them were sons born after the flood." The next five verses list the sons and grandsons of Japheth. Verse 6 tells us that Ham had four sons: "And the sons of Ham: Cush, and Mizraim, and Phut, and Canaan." Then verse 8 focuses in on one particular son of Ham, that is, Cush. Read these words very carefully: "And Cush begat Nimrod; he began to be a mighty one in the earth. He was a mighty hunter before the Lord, . . . And the beginning of his kingdom was Babel, ..." (Most marginal references read "Babylon.")

Are you thinking that you might have Charlie's problem right now? A real build-up and no thundering revelations? Do you feel like you missed something? Did you miss something? No great discovery in those few words? Well, join the group.

You see, without two additional elements you will naturally miss it. One is the historical accounts of this man Nimrod and the other is the change in meaning from the original Hebrew language Genesis was written in. Without a long and boring list of historical quotations, let me briefly fill you in. Since this is so fantastic and almost unbelievably shocking, you will find a listing of books at the end of this book for substantiation and additional reading. But, here goes.

After Noah and his family finished their trip of safety in the ark life had to begin almost all over again. There was no vegetation at first. As a matter of fact, there was nothing but miles and miles of nothing. The Creator provided the basics for new life through the contents of the ark. As this life started anew, one man began to stand out above others. His name was Nimrod. You just read where he started a kingdom . . . Babylon. Historians contribute the origination of the concept of cities to Nimrod. Wild beasts

19

developed through their wilderness existence and became an ever-increasing danger to family life. Nimrod clustered some families together in small bands which he defended himself. So the reason is clear why the Bible says that Nimrod "began to be a mighty hunter."

You know that the book of Genesis was written in the Hebrew language. The King James Version is a translation of Hebrew into English, in the Old Testament, and from Greek into English in the New Testament.

When the President of the United States visits most countries he must employ a translator to convey his message to the leaders and people of those foreign places. The King James Version is much like that. It is a foreign language being translated into our language so we can understand the message.

Now, as it is the case in the translators trying to convey the message of the President of the United States in other languages, sometimes a word will lose some of its impact and importance. It is too bad, but nevertheless, it happens quite frequently.

In this short account of Noah's family tree one such word is tragically losing its impact and importance. That word is the key to opening up a whole new perspective and a thrilling discovery.

It is this statement, "He was a mighty hunter before the Lord." The key word is "before." The casual reading gives you the impression that Nimrod was a mighty hunter "in the eyes of the Lord," or "before His presence." Actually the Hebrew renders it something to the effect that Nimrod was a mighty hunter "in place of" the Lord. In the seventeenth century English language the word "before" actually meant more like "against" or "instead of." A man was said to have preferred owning a horse "before" a mule. He wanted the horse in place of the mule. It was the man's first preference. In the case of Nimrod history substantiates the fact that the word "before" actually should have read "in place of."

20

As Nimrod used his God-given talents and strength to protect the people he had clustered together in little bands, he acquired the admiration and appreciation of the people he defended.

One of the most amazing things happened to Nimrod. To be accepted is wonderful, to be appreciated is grand, to be honored is thrilling, but, to be worshipped is blasphemous. That is, for a man to be worshipped by other humans is a terrible sin.

In an almost perfect miniature reproduction of the great rebellion in Heaven, the admiration and respect started to do things within the mind of Nimrod. He, too, started his own worship services as he gazed upon his own physique. Satan, sensing a sensational opportunity, added to the ego of Nimrod.

A friend of mine has done an extensive and exhaustive study into the ways and means the Creator speaks to His creatures. Briefly, it is his belief that it all occurs through electrical impulses to the brain. Whatever the method may be, the highly intelligent fallen angel is very much aware of that method too. So, he speaks to you just about in the same way God does. That is why mankind has always been plagued by "two different voices" speaking to him and making impressions. Whatever scientific manner it might have been Satan still added to the ego of Nimrod by repeating again and again into his willing ear of the greatness and wisdom Nimrod possessed. Nimrod became the dupe of the devil.

It was not very long after the establishment of the Babylonian kingdom under Nimrod that Nimrod allowed his followers to hail him as a god! Nimrod became a "mighty hunter in the place of God."

Since many scholars interpret the word "before" as being "against", and since the Jewish Encyclopedia states unequivocally that Nimrod was the one who made the people turn away from God, the word "against" is the better translation. As you will see, through Satan's suggestions, Nimrod and his wife did turn millions and millions against God!

21

Not only behind every good man stands a good woman, but in most cases behind every bad man there is also an equally bad woman. Nimrod was no exception. The woman standing behind Nimrod was Semiramis. Since Nimrod became the king and later the god, Semiramis was also the queen and another god. Both king and queen were worshipped. Nimrod, though king, finally went the way of all men. He died. The queen desperately kept the kingdom together. Through satanic inspiration, the queen called her kingdom together. The events that took place on the day of that convocation have forever afterwards altered man's relationship with the Creator!

Babylon . . . Babel . . . the Bible speaks many, many times about this city and kingdom. In all the prophetic books (books dealing with prophecy), Babylon is used to represent the total kingdom of the Devil. It is the epitome of everything opposite and opposed to God. The city of Jerusalem represents everything good and in harmony with God's teachings. The two names, Jerusalem and Babylon, are represented as the two direct opposites of good and evil, truth and error, life and death.

The declarations of the Queen of Babylon on that day of her kingdom's united assembly will prove to show why God has used Babylon throughout the Bible to represent Satan's word and works.

The entire kingdom stood before the palace. They anxiously anticipated some great event to take place that day. It did.

The queen made her majestic appearance to the enthralled crowd. Tension could be cut with a knife. What was to happen to the kingdom now that the king was dead? They hoped for a real solution. The queen lifted her arms for the crowd to stop their cheers. That gigantic mass became silent. Then Queen Semiramis announced to the spellbound throng one of the most dumbfounding and desecrating declarations ever made against the Diety!

She announced to her followers that the gods of the sky

22

had revealed to her that their great and beloved king was now serving his people in an exalted position. Nimrod was now the sun-god! She vividly and enthusiastically described how he had been elevated to this place to give them greater protection than ever before.

The description was then painted of the earth being a flat, round shape like that of our modern-day dinner plate. With astonishing adjectives and stunning superlatives, the queen described to the breathless crowd how beneath the earth, on the bottom side, were all manner of gigantic, devouring demons trying to creep and crawl up over the edge to destroy them. Now Nimrod was not only going to fight and keep back the demons as he plunged over the edge of the world at the end of the day, but he was also going to doubly insure that they receive warmth and light at day. He was truly an even greater protector and provider than when he was there in person. The sun-god!

The sun . . . the moon . . . the stars . . . all gods!

The sun . . . the moon . . . the stars . . . very visible gods.

The sun . . . the moon . . . the stars . . . tangible proof of their existence.

To those ancient minds assembled before the queen in her luxury and luster all this was not far-fetched. Where did the sun go every day? Now they had the answer! Semiramis' satanic spell has succeeded. They accepted the story because they could see something in the sky each day and that bright ball of fire was not something superstitious anymore but the sun-god sending down blessings on his people! Then, when it disappeared it was going to war for them against those subterranean evil spirits and demons. When it came up again in the sky they knew that they had another day of safety. It all made sense.

In an equally demonstrative declaration the queen now appealed to their emotions! In deepest gratitude they were to now demonstrate their devotion to Nimrod by falling prostrate before him as he made his victorious appearance

23

every morning fresh from battle! The queen laid down the rules for this new form of worship. Every man, woman, and child were to bow before the sun every morning and give thanks. So began the satanic practice of sun-worship. A sinister substitute, a counterfeit religion, and you are going to be amazed at the ways and means Satan has perpetrated this anti-Christian practice through the centuries. Yet, consider more.

Approximately two to three years after Nimrod's death and the institution of sun-worship a very unusual and unorthodox event took place within the palace. The queen is found to be in the early stages of motherhood. Again the vast kingdom is called together for another great convocation. This time the announcement of one of the most stunning and startling claims ever made by a human being. Once Satan takes control of the human mind there is almost no limit to which he can take that controlled mind. Semiramis was an outstanding example. Standing before that sprawling multitude the adulterous and idolatrous queen proclaims that she has been richly blessed by receiving a child from the sun-god, Nimrod! It is the direct product of divine intervention. She declares that the sperm from Nimrod came through the rays of the sun. Though is was Semiramis' voice making those blasphemous decrees, it was Satan's schemes all the way.

The convocation continued. The proud queen made another decree. Since the sun was worshipped, his direct descendant was to be also. Since her child was a god-product, she, then, was a "mother of god!" Satan used one man, Nimrod, and his wife, Semiramis, as human tools through which to begin a long, long reign of counterfeit religions and false doctrines.

In establishing sun-worship he laid the foundation of all cults, false gods, and anti-Biblical teachings. As you see how Satan builds on his foundation, you will see the world wide hoax unfold more and more in amazing event after event.

But, brace yourself. You might see something along the way that you have innocently fallen victim to. You might even discover more than one concept you have sincerely felt was a perfectly correct Christian concept all along. Yes, you might be in for a few surprises!

3/INVASION

As you will see, Satan used every conceivable and confounding instrument available to try to completely conceal from mankind the true, holy, pure character, and unselfish love of God. As you delve into the depths of the Devil's deceptive and destructive deeds against Deity, you will begin to see how easily mankind was to fall for the swindle of all swindles. But, a little warning first! As these stunning steps of Satan are exposed you might very well expect to have a few personal shocks along the way.

Whatever your concepts of the Biblical recounting of a certain minister being swallowed by a large fish may be, modern experiences have shown that it not only could be true but very feasible. Too many such incidents have been recorded as documented facts today to throw out the story of Jonah and the whale. By the way, you probably already know that in the original Hebrew it did render the words "huge fish" instead of "whale." Nevertheless, the reason for the preacher, Jonah, having that traumatic trip in the fish was his refusal to take a specified voyage to a center of sun worship.

Nineveh was a city of nearly a quarter of a million people. Almost every man, woman, and child was actively involved in the gross perversions taking place under the teachings of sun worship. Jonah was commissioned to go to that city and tell the over two hundred thousand population about the true God of Creation. Jonah was terrified at the order. Everywhere in the sprawling ancient city were visible gods of worship. The Ninevites had plunged to the depths of satanic mythology and mysticism. Jonah was overwhelmed with the odds against his one-man campaign against the most sinister and perverted power known at that time. He tried to dodge the issue by taking a route away from, instead of towards, Nineveh. The rest of the story is history. Jonah did go to Nineveh. His success has never been equaled in the history of preaching. Nineveh experienced a temporary revival. Yet, eventually it did go back to the pagan practices that led Jonah there in the first place.

The swallowing of Jonah by a large fish is a fantastic event in the annals of the history of the Creator directly intervening in the affairs of humanity. But, even more amazing than that is the legend that originated in ancient Nineveh itself.

When Nineveh had become a relatively large city, a so-called governmental system was established. It was an attempt to make the city run in an orderly fashion. A city charter was formed. Unlike our American Constitution, religious liberty was not guaranteed. Sun worship was an integral part of its code, and from that code comes this legend that you are going to be stunned by as you read it.

Two things are absolutely amazing about this myth, this legend. The first one is that it was created over two thousand years before Christ. You will see why this is important as it is unfolded to you. The second aspect that is even more amazing is the fact that not only has this pagan practice been kept alive all these thirty-nine centuries but the role many Christians have played in keeping it so well and alive!

Brace yourself! Here goes.

It seems that the ancient Ninevites looked up into the sky one day as they heard the sound of some type of missle streaking towards the earth. The ever-descending object was a gigantic egg! It fell directly into the Euphrates River and down onto the river's floor. It did not even crack. The legend says that after the egg had softly settled down on the bottom of the river a large school of fish came to the egg and rolled it up onto the shore away from the water. (Did you picture people participating in an innocent little custom of ":egg-rolling?") Then it seems that a certain select group of doves flew down to the egg. Easing their bodies gently down on the egg they sat on the egg until the warmth of their collective bodies hatched it. And the fable describes that the egg started to crack wide open and out of this huge egg came the Goddess of the Moon! Her name was Ishtar. And, believe it or not, it is from her name, Ishtar, that the name "Easter" originated!

Are you starting to have the same kind of uneasy feeling as I did when reading this fable? If not, maybe you will as you read more.

Ishtar, the Moon Goddess, was supposed to have given birth to a son through the same miraculous sperm-like "ray from the sun" as did Queen Semiramis. This son's birth was hailed as a divine, "immaculate conception." The story tells that his name was "Tamaz." In the King James Bible it is spelled "Tammuz." Nevertheless, you can easily see how Satan was able, to a certain successful degree, to take away from the power and force of the actual virgin birth of Christ by coming up with this widely accepted legend some two thousand years before.

Get this! This purely pagan misconception goes on to profoundly state that this "divinely conceived" son, Tamaz, was supposed to have been born on the twenty-fifth day of December!

And if that were not enough, this satanically inspired fable tells that this son was later killed by a wild boar, and, look at this, the son was supposed to have been resurrected from the dead by the power of the sun god three days later!

His "resurrection" was supposed to have taken place on "the first day of the first week after the vernal equinox," or on "the first Sun-day after the full moon that occurs on, or about, March the twenty-first!" Then, a yearly celebration

28

followed. This annual event became a national holiday. Each year these sun worshippers would pay homage to the death of Tamaz. They observed his death by going through a period of self-affliction imitating his suffering. This was done by "weeping and fasting for forty days before his resurrection day."

This really threw me for a loop when I realized that today in modern Christianity there is a forty-day period of doing without some specified items, and that time of abstinence is called "Lent."

When the sun worshippers had passed this forty days of doing without certain food items, they would then go through another amazing ritual. Three days after Tamaz was supposed to have been killed, very early in the morning before dawn, the sun worshippers would go out of town to a certain gathering place and wait for the sun to rise as proof of his resurrection!

During these heathen convocations these followers of heavenly, celestial gods would make little round cakes for "the Queen of Heaven." They indented the rising dough with their fingers so as to make a plus mark, a pagan symbol of fertility, across the entire top of the miniature cake. These cakes were taken up into the mountain tops later in the day. They were placed out before the noon sun and eaten warm as a part of their ritual to the sun.

There is no need to say this. You have probably already thought of it, but a similar cake is known today as a hot cross bun!

In two outstanding passages in the Bible are found God's recorded open statement of displeasure over these rituals. Many people do not know that these stunning statements are even in the Bible. One is in Jeremiah 7:17-20. It is the Lord speaking to Jeremiah and it goes like this, "Seeth thou not what they do in the cities of Judah and in the streets of Jerusalem? The children gather wood, and the fathers kindle the fire, and the women knead their dough, to make cakes to the queen of heaven, and to pour out drink offerings unto other gods, that they may provoke me to anger. Do they provoke me to anger? saith the Lord. Do not they provoke themselves to the confusion of their own faces? Therefore thus saith the Lord God, Behold mine anger and my fury shall be poured out upon this place, upon man, and upon beast, and upon the trees of the field, and upon the fruit of the ground; and it shall burn, and shall not be quenched.''

Many deep Bible students feel that it may very well be that the crop failures, droughts, floods, and other such agriculture related problems of today could be a direct result of the continuing practices of these ''innocent rituals.''

The second astounding statement of the Creator regarding these pagan observances is found in Ezekiel 8:13-16. Once again the Creator is talking to another human. The human is Ezekiel and the conversation goes this way, ''And He said unto me, turn thee yet again and thou shalt see greater abominations that they do. Then He brought me to the door of the gate of the Lord's house which was toward the North; and, behold, there sat women weeping for Tammuz! Then said He unto me, hast thou seen this, O son of man? Turn thee yet again (in other words, take another look), and thou shall see greater abominations than these. And He brought me into the inner court of the Lord's house (right inside), and, behold, at the door of the temple of the Lord, between the porch and the altar, were about five and twenty men, with their backs toward the temple of the Lord, and their faces toward the East, and they worshipped the sun toward the East!'' Then the verses that follow this repeat God's definite displeasure over sun worship.

In the realm of Christianity there are certain specific standards and truths. Just as there is no deviation in other laws of God, there can be no deviation from truth and standards. Two plus two still makes four. These truths and standards can be placed into 18 segments. There are 18 divisions in Christian doctrine. When you take the Bible and break down these divisions you will have 18 basic communiques from the Creator to His creations. Eighteen messages from the Master to mankind. The finest and most sincere minister will speak every week to his congregation. If he does so for 25 years, he will still have only covered about 18 basic doctrines if he covers all Bible truth.

Now, please notice this. For every one Bible truth Satan has a counterfeit, a lie! Each one of his counterfeit doctrines has its basis in pagan sun worship.

Eighteen counterfeit teachings! Modern man would not accept the outright perversion of Bible fact. Satan knows this full well. He is very much aware that no thinking human being, in his right mind, would believe the gross substitutes over and above the revealed Word of God. So, the scheme? A mingling of lies with the truth! Mix sun worship into Christianity and you will wind up with a watered-down social concept! Blend sun worship into Christianity and you have a powerful perversion of principle. Get Christianity to accept sun worship and the blend will give you a direct diversion from the Divine directions.

In just a few short pages you have already seen how this could really succeed if it is carried to the complete Christian concept. You have seen the origin of such innocent little rituals as egg-rolling, hot cross buns, and sun-rise services, to mention a few. Through the years, the equally innocent customs of painting eggs in bright colors, egg hunts, Easter bunnies, and many other harmless myths have grown out of this same legend. These myths are minor and insignificant. But, in the pages to follow you are going to see Biblical and historical proof that this same type of sun worship psychology has slipped slowly, but silently, into the church to the very point that it has, and is, endangering the fibers of the foundation of Christianity. You will see astonishing examples of this sinister counterfeit actually turning millions and millions of honest, dependable, and earnest men and women away from the once well-founded trust and respect for religion and holy things.

The dean of the school of engineering at a large American university discovered in a lecture series the things you just read. He sought out a good friend who was also a professor at the same university. The other professor was also a

31

sincere Sunday School teacher and very knowledgeable in history. The dean asked the Christian professor if the rituals of egg-rolling, Lent, Easter eggs, and sunrise services were actually pagan.

The professor replied, "Oh sure they're pagan all right, but we've Christianized them!"

Could this same "Christianizing" of sun worshipping theories and practices be the ways and means of Lucifer's worldwide hoax becoming an accepted reality?

4/THE LAYMAN'S CHALLENGE

A close relative lie dying in bed at home. I had driven nearly two hundred miles to visit him. After talking to the rest of the family I made my way to the rear of his home where a hospital bed had been placed so he would not only be comfortable but isolated from most of the noise. He had lost weight but was cheerful. We exchanged greetings and talked about my children. Before I could inquire into his condition another visitor came in. I was kind of surprised to see this man, but I was to be even more surprised by a question he was to later ask.

This tall, slender, middle-aged man had once been a member of the denomination in which I was a pastor. He had left the denomination we were in to unite with a group I considered radical.

It was a little uncomfortable with this man standing on the opposite side of the patient's bed. I had often thought about what I would say to him if the opportunity ever came. Now he was right there and I wondered if I would have the chance to say something to him. You see, he had turned his back on some things I had been taught all my life as being reliable certainties. I really felt he had turned from a faith and trust in the saving power of Christ, and was now attempting to bring about his own salvation through works. Ministers call those kind of people "legalists."

The conversation was typical. Then the visitor said something that caused the patient to ask him why he had made such a drastic change. The quiet and calm visitor replied, "I changed because I discovered the truth. I want to base all my beliefs and practices on the Bible and the Bible only."

That was my chance! So, I let this man have both barrels. "If you really believed the Bible you would be back with us observing the Lord's day and not that old Jewish Sabbath."

No tact, my words were more like an attack! But, it did not shake him in the least. He smiled, looked down at my relative, and then turned his attention directly towards me. He just looked at me in a very calm way.

I didn't give him time to say anything else. "I preach twice every Sunday. I observe Sunday as the holy day of rest and worship because that's the day Christ rose from the dead. The Bible tells us to honor His resurrection by going to church on Sunday," I said in a real authoritative manner that should have ended the whole thing. But it didn't!

He smiled and said, "Bill, I wish you would give me just one text to prove what you just said."

The next two or three minutes seemed like an eternity. I just could not think of one single text. I was embarrassed. "I . . . I . . . I can't think of one off the top of my head. If I had brought my Bible with me I'd give you five or six texts."

I was even more embarrassed when the kind challenger reached into his coat pocket and produced a small New Testament. I fumbled through the gospels, the book of Acts, and several other New Testament books but nothing popped out at me from off the pages. I felt four eyes staring at me. Both men were silent. My relative sensed my difficulty and said, "It's strange how, when you're looking for something in the Bible and know it well, you can never seem to find it. Like trying to find a cop when you need one," and laughed.

"Well, I wish I had lots of time," I said, "And didn't have to drive two hundred miles tonight, but, I'll look them all up and mail you a long, long list." I said good night to both of them and walked out.

In my car I felt terrible. I had not only NOT had prayer with my relative, but I had revealed my lack of knowledge of the Bible. Here I was a minister, and a layman had tripped me up. It was a long ride back, and I asked the Lord to forgive me for not being able to stand up for the truth, and promised Him I would really study more.

"There is a difference in having something to preach about, and having to preach about something;" a prominent minister once confessed. The pressure of having to produce two helpful sermons every Sunday is sometimes very strong. So, I spent lots of time in my study searching for sermon material. Once I got the thought, the goal, the message I wanted to get across settled in my mind the long process began. After completely typing the sermon out on paper I would "preach" it into a tape recorder. That would take care of Sunday morning's message. Then the same routine for Sunday night. I usually tried to do this early in the mornings leaving the afternoons for visitation. When I had my first sermon completed I would take the small recorder with me and listen to it every chance I got. Sometimes I would listen to it as much as twelve times. Then on Saturday mornings I would go back down to the office, make notes from that Sunday morning sermon, and place the notes, or outline, in a small three ring notebook. I would preach from that notebook.

Sunday afternoon, as soon as I could gulp down a meal, I would go to the office and make the notes for the evening service, listening to the sermon on the recorder as many times as I could. The sermon preparation was a pressure all right, maybe too much.

Because of being out of town that week the pressure was very much present the next morning. Vowing to myself that I would look up those texts after finishing the first sermon, I soon forgot about the challenge. At least for awhile.

In addition to preaching two sermons on Sunday and

one on Wednesday nights, I also taught a Sunday School class of young adults. It was an easy class because the questions and discussions always went in every direction. You did not have to study the lesson quarterlies very much. This particular Sunday I was more appreciative of that fact. I had not time to even look at the subject in the young adult class's quarterly except hastily. I led into a discussion hoping that the class would get so involved in loving debates that the time would fly by. But, it backfired!

In the middle of a good discussion one of the young married men turned to me and asked, "Pastor, how come we go to church on Sunday when the Bible says that the seventh day is the Sabbath? Isn't the seventh day Saturday?"

For a second or two my mind flashed back before me a picture of that kind visitor's challenge a few days earlier, and, of course, that terrible feeling of embarrassment I experienced.

"Well," I replied, "The Jewish people were given the seventh day Sabbath at Mount Sinai for them only. The Sabbath is a Jewish institution. Now that we are no longer under those old Jewish laws of works and are under grace, we observe a new day." I really tried to make up for that failure a few days before. "You see," I continued, "The Jews looked forward in faith to the Messiah. We look back in faith to the Lord Jesus Christ. Jesus died on Friday. He rested in the tomb on the seventh day, the Sabbath, to show us that it was no longer in effect. Then He arose from the grave on the first day, Sunday, to institute a new memorial!"

Just as I started to say that the Bible talks a lot about the first day of the week being the new day, I remembered that bedside challenge. I eased out of it, changed the subject, and hoped that the bell signaling the end of the class time would sound off!

Maybe those two incidents, coming so close together, were the Lord's way of making me aware of a situation that demanded attention. Maybe there were some people in my church who had questions about the New Testament

36

day of worship. Maybe the Lord was leading me to preach on the subject. Maybe He was trying to show me how I needed to spend some more time on my individual study and less on my sermons. Anyway, I knew I had to deal with the subject once and for all.

Martin Luther had once declared that it was to be the "Bible and Bible only," as the rule of faith for the Christians. So, before reading what other ministers and scholars had written about the subject, I knew I had to see exactly what the Bible revealed. I wanted to be fair even though I knew that over two hundred and fifty different denominations could not all be wrong. They all keep Sunday and have no questions whatsoever about it. I guess I just wanted to try to be fair.

The Bible teaches that this earth has been in existence now about six thousand years. It teaches that the earth came into existence by an act of special creation and not from an evolutionary process. The biggest majority of denominations are in agreement with this. Also they are in complete harmony that there were six literal days of creation week, and each of these days were 24 hours in duration. So, I went to the first book of the Bible, Genesis, to reread the accounts of that creation of earth.

In Genesis 2:1-3 are recorded these words, "Thus the heavens and the earth were finished, and all the host of them. And on the seventh day God ended His work which He had made. And God rested on the seventh day from all His work which He had made. And God blessed the seventh day and sanctified it, because that in it He had rested from all His work which God created and made." Okay, this was the establishment of the weekly cycle. There were to be seven days in each week. At creation the Lord set aside the very last day of that week to be a memorial to His creation. It said that He "sanctified" that day. When I looked up the meaning of that word I found that it was to "set apart for a holy use, or to make holy." So the Lord made one day "holy." It was to be a special day for man. It was an outstanding day in which the man

He made was to stop his hustle and bustle in life, and zero in on the One who gave him that life. It was to be a time of definite physical rest and spiritual refreshment. It was to have been a time when the Creator would come very close to His creations, and share a special time of peace.

That all made sense. After all, that was what I had been telling my people all along about the Lord's day. Sunday was to be different from all the other working days.

Many times I had stated in sermons that the Bible mentions many times in this story of the establishment of a holy day "God" or "He" or "His." And I stressed those references were there about creation week to let us know that God had established the system of working six days and then making the seventh one the Lord's special day! We could not get away from the fact it was God's original plan and not man's.

God established a special day for man. All through the Old Testament I found this fact repeated over and over again. When the Jewish nation came into being they were told to adopt that special day, too. There was no way I could deny that the Jews kept the Sabbath holy!

But, now we are in New Testament times. We are now under grace. So, I had to find the proof of Sunday in the New Testament. My search was fantastic!

I advertised that our church worshipped on "The Lord's day." I even had one text to substantiate that placed in a prominent place in the church bulletin and newsletter. That text is Revelation 1:10. You know it. Everyone uses it. It goes like this: "I was in the spirit on the Lord's day and heard behind me a great voice, as of a trumpet." I read the verses before this, and after, but there was no mention of any particular day. "Everyone knows the Lord's day is Sunday," I said to myself.

But then I looked into the history of this verse. John was the writer. He was an apostle of Jesus Christ. He had been banished to a barren, volcanic island in the Aegean Sea. It was in the Apenal colony of the Romans. He was isolated on this waste land because of his refusal to stop telling everyone about the Risen Lord. He said that he was there on a certain day when he was "in the spirit," or was given a vision. He called that day "the Lord's day." But I had to admit that in this one verse John did not actually say what day it is.

Since the term "the Lord's day" is used by most Christians to designate Sunday, surely "the Lord" would know! So, I started looking at each of the verses in which Jesus had spoken of a day of rest and worship.

I had a book before me that listed every single word in the Bible and the exact chronological order in which they were found. It not only listed each word, but it told where I could find the first time it was used, then the second, then the third, and so on. Imagine my surprise when the very first time Jesus spoke of a day of worship and rest did not even use the term "the Lord's day!" It is Matthew 12:8 and Jesus said this, "The Son of Man is Lord even of the Sabbath day."

Looking at the context, the setting in which He said this, I saw He was talking to some Jewish religious leaders. They kept the Sabbath in stricter ways than God intended. They criticized Jesus and His disciples for walking through a wheat field and, as they went, plucked some grain in their hands, rubbing them together to knock off the hard outer shells. They did this on the Sabbath day. The leaders said that the disciples and Jesus had violated the Sabbath. So Jesus reminded them that God made the Sabbath in the beginning and, as God's son, He was Lord of the Sabbath too. In other words, Jesus knew full well that it was an holy day and that He and His disciples had not broken the sanctity in any way. They were snacking, so to speak, and not harvesting a crop!

Even though I had always thought of Sunday every time I read this verse, Jesus was talking about that day that was still in effect then. He was talking about the seventh-day Sabbath. But, He knew it was going to be changed after awhile. Maybe He didn't say anything about that change to those leaders then because He wanted to do it after He had

39

been resurrected. They would surely accept His changing a day when they had seen Him miraculously come out of the tomb alive!

My book told me that the first day of the week was definitely mentioned in the very next passage dealing with a day of worship, but so was the Sabbath. It is Matthew 28:1, and goes like this: "In the end of the Sabbath, as it began to dawn toward the first day of the week, came Mary Magdalene and the other Mary to see the sepulchre (the grave)." That was all? Just an historical account of the resurrection? It tells of Mary and her friends going out to the grave of Jesus on Sunday morning all right, but what was said about it being changed now to replace the seventh day? The verses before and after this make no mention of the Lord wanting us to observe the first day of the week in honor of those miraculous happenings there that day. But, this was only the second reference. I would find it in the others, or at least some of the other passages.

The Bible states that "An honest confession is good for the soul." Let me make one to you right now. After I started on this Biblical research program I had to come face to face with the fact that I had been preaching to sincere people in the pews of my church urging them to know the Bible. I urged their attendance on Wednesday nights so they would learn more about the book we all call the Word of God. And, yet, here I was coming to the realization that I did not know very much about that Word of God! On several occasions I had felt very hypocritical. This research was revealing a lot about myself.

When I was in the seminary, a small salary and three young children made me realize that when I needed dependable transportation I was limited in my choices. A trip to the library to look through car magazines let me know that there were only a few in my price range. So I studied the pros and cons of those cars. I eventually caught a train to the factory and picked up my new car there to cut down the costs.

As a general rule I investigate a book thoroughly before

buying it. I like to read the headings of the chapters, look at any pictures, and look at the description of the author.

When it comes to buying beautiful suits my track record is very bad. So my wife, bless her heart, agrees to go along and supervise. Her knowledge of material, quality, and good taste never fails. Maybe you might feel that this is lowering the standards of man hood, but, remember this, a wife will never criticize your suit if she picked it out.

But, I generally investigate most other things, and as I was studying I began to wonder why I had not investigated this matter? I was taking many things for granted and placing a great deal of trust in others.

In the New Testament four books are dedicated to the relating to man the major events in Christ's ministry for mankind. Those are, of course, Matthew, Mark, Luke and John. Each writer's views, added to the others, gives an over-all picture that only one writer could not possibly do. So, in comparing the four gospels you can pretty well establish the truth about some of the actions and concepts of the Lord. Surely it was His plan to preserve the history in this manner. I had to do the same thing—compare.

In the book of Matthew I did not find anything to prove to my friend that Sunday was the correct day for Christians to observe now. I had to find it in the other gospel books.

Mark's book speaks of both the Sabbath and the first day. In Mark 16:1–2, the next chronological passage, I read this: ''And when the Sabbath was past, Mary Magdalene, and Mary the mother of James, and Salome, had brought sweet spices, that they might come and anoint Him. And very early in the morning, the first day of the week, they came unto the sepulchre at the rising of the sun.'' This is basically the same story Matthew told. I saw that it was just another historical account of the resurrection morning. I was getting a little impatient. When would someone go on and say something about ''the old Sabbath,'' or ''the Jewish Sabbath,'' or ''the Sabbath of the old

41

dispensation," or "the Sabbath of the old covenant," as many other ministers and I referred to the Sabbath?

In the sixteenth chapter of Mark there is something else mentioning the first day of the week. It is verse 9, and says, "Now when Jesus was risen early the first day of the week, He appeared first to Mary Magdalene, out of whom He had cast seven devils." Again there was nothing. The first two gospel books weren't helping me at all.

The thought flashed through my mind, "Maybe the Lord didn't use the term 'the first day of the week' at all when He changed the day. Maybe He referred to the 'resurrection day', or something like that. Maybe that was the reason for my friend acting so calmly. Maybe he had done this same research and was tripping me up over semantics! Do you think he knew the change was there all right, but the Lord didn't use the term 'the Lord's day' when He made it?"

When I hurried on over into the book of Luke I discovered something I had never realized was in the Bible. It was Luke 23:54 and it was this: "And that day was the preparation, and the Sabbath drew on." Luke said that the Sabbath was drawing on, or soon to begin. Since the Jewish Sabbath was on Saturday, the seventh day, Luke had to be talking about something taking place on Friday, the sixth day. He was calling Friday the Jewish preparation day. I wondered to myself, "preparation for what?"

I had to turn for outside help. In doing so I learned that since the Jews were not supposed to do any regular work during the hours of their Sabbath, and since it was to be different from the other common six days, and since certain restrictions were placed on their activities on that day, then certain "preparations" had to have been done prior to the start of their holy day of rest.

The ladies made sure that their family wash was all done, the ironing completed, the baking finished, the meals prepared, the house cleaned, and everything about the home in such an order that there would be a peaceful, calm, neat and congenial atmosphere for the family to begin its family worship.

The men finished their work, closed their businesses, completed their chores, got haircuts if necessary, and made sure they were home in time to leisurely take their baths before leading out in the family's observance of their holy day.

The children even prepared for the Sabbath. They put away their normal weekly toys, cleaned their rooms, took their baths, selected their clothes for church, and found their places in the family circle.

The "preparation" or "preparation day" was everything its name implied. It was the loving acts of sincere believers to help make their Sabbath a holy day, sacred and enjoyable. It was not just a day to go to church, but a day for the honest-of-heart Jew to set aside all secular work, talk, and activities so his mind and heart could focus in on the Lord. To the dedicated Jew it was not just a day for physical rest, but also a day for spiritual refreshment and reviving.

I remember how my mind wandered to the average member's treatment of the new day of rest and worship. As soon as we finished church on Sunday most of us would make a beeline to a cafeteria close to our church. We even had a little game among three other ministers in the area as to which congregation would get in line first after we had preached. The last group in line "must have had a long-winded preacher," we'd say to each other.

Sunday afternoon was a variety of things from football on television to 18 holes of golf. I thought about so many of our members missing an occasional service because they worked that day. But, most of the members, regardless of what they did on Sunday afternoon, were right back in church for the evening worship service. I kind of wondered how it would be if we Christians were a little more protective of our activities on the Lord's day like the Jews were of their Sabbath. Maybe if we had a "preparation day" things might be different.

After that thought-provoking discovery I read the rest of

the passage. In Luke 23:54, and going on into the twenty-fourth chapter, this information about the first day is given, "And the women also, which came with Him from Galilee, followed after, and beheld the sepulchre, and how His body was lain. And they returned and prepared spices and ointments; and rested the Sabbath day, according to the commandment. Now, upon the first day of the week, very early in the morning, they came unto the sepulchre, bringing the spices which they had prepared, and certain others with them. And they found the stone rolled away from the sepulchre."

It did not take me long to recognize that this was repeating almost the same report about the believers finding the grave empty. But I got another insight that really was interesting.

Maybe you noticed this, too. The other writers had not brought it out, had they? Did you notice that these believers skipped thirty-six hours in their process of preparing the body of Jesus for death? They went out to the grave on Friday afternoon, the preparation day. They found His body in the grave. They looked at the clothes given to Him by Joseph and Nicodemus when they placed Him in Joseph's tomb. Then they went home and got all the spices and ointments prepared before their Sabbath started. By the way, the Jewish Sabbath was observed from sundown on Friday to sundown Saturday. The Bible counted time from sunset on one day to sunset the next. So, the women had to hurry and get finished before the sun set on Friday. But why did they wait until Sunday morning before coming back out to finish the embalming process?

"Sure," I decided, "They knew that Sunday was the new day. Jesus was going to rise in three days and they were going to go back out and celebrate His resurrection." But, my second thought shot that theory to pieces. "They didn't know that Jesus was going to rise again. They wouldn't have made any preparations if they had known He was going to come out of that tomb in three days alive! They didn't even know the Scriptures well enough to

44

recognize Him as the Saviour, know why He was going to the cross, much less know He was going to be victorious over death."

Why did they waste thirty-six hours? Since the Bible is its own commentary, I reread the passage to get the answer. It states that they went home and prepared the spices and ointments and then "rested the Sabbath day according to the commandment."

The commandment was the fourth one that said, "Remember the Sabbath day to keep it holy. Six days shalt thou labor and do all thy work, but the seventh day is the Sabbath of the Lord thy God . . ." They rested because they did not recognize a change in God's law, and particularly the fourth commandment. They must have felt it was still in effect as far as they were concerned. They prepared the spices on Friday before the end of the day, before sunset. But, they refused to do any work on the Sabbath, even to pay their last respects to the Lord. They were strict in their observance of the Sabbath, but I felt that this was carrying things too far!

Matthew, Mark, and Luke were not coming up with that one text for me. I was going to give my friend several, but I would settle for one right now.

But, the next reference gave me some relief. I knew that eventually I was going to come up with the texts. At last, in John's gospel there is the story of the disciples in their first recorded assembly together on Sunday. It is one of the foundations on which Sunday worship rests. "How could I have forgotten this one? How come I couldn't remember this twentieth chapter of John at that bedside?"

Here it is. John 20:19: "Then the same day at evening, being the first day of the week, when the doors were shut where the disciples were assembled for fear of the Jews, came Jesus and stood in the midst, and saith unto them, Peace be unto you."

Before this, every passage of scripture dealing with the first day of the week centered in around events before the resurrection. Now comes a passage dealing with a meeting

45

that took place Sunday night. The night following Christ's resurrection and a meeting of His followers was taking place. How about that, I finally got to something concrete. John 20:19 was the verse I had been seeking. Surely there were more too!

I was really relieved. I guess my pride had been hurt and I was embarrassed by my inability to quote, or even to find, Bible verses to prove my beliefs. I was so happy I reread the verse to memorize it. I wanted to be able to quote it perfectly. "Then the same day (the resurrection day) at evening, being the first day of the week," I read out loud, "When the doors were shut where the disciples were assembled for fear of the Jews. . . ." Wait a minute, they were assembled for what? I read it again, "when the doors were shut, where the disciples were assembled for fear of the Jews . . ." My jubilation died. Man, how come I never saw that before? Those disciples weren't there holding a worship service. They weren't mapping out missionary projects. They weren't deciding on a name for their new church. They were there because they thought they might be next to go to the cross or prison. They had seen what the religious leaders had done to Jesus. They had been His closest associates all that time. The disciples were there because of "fear of the Jews" and I just never, ever even read it much less grasped its significance!

That word "fear" just jumped out at me! I don't know why I did it, but I looked up the word "fear" to see what it meant in its original Greek. You realize that the New Testament was written in Greek. The King James Bible translates the Greek into English so we can understand. I looked up the word "fear" and it comes from the word "phobos." "Phobos" is where we get the word "phobia." And you know that "phobia" means "an intense horror." These disciples were there because they were terrified of what might happen next. They were trying to work out a solution. They were meeting behind closed doors because of their fear. That is exactly why Jesus came into their midst and said, "Peace be unto you." He wanted to calm

46

their fears by announcing to them of His resurrection. I wondered, as I saw this explosive and shaking passage, how many other ministers I knew were aware of this.

Tolstoy wrote: "Man must not check reason by tradition, but contrariwise, must check tradition by reason." I knew good and well that Jesus had changed the Sabbath into Sunday, and I just wanted to close my Bible and forget trying to prove it to my friend. After all, I had more important things to do than to sit around trying to prove someone right and someone wrong. What difference did it make anyway? After all, every day ought to be a holy day to the Lord! Just as long as I keep one day, what difference does it make? The Lord looks at your sincerity anyway.

But, maybe it was the thought of seeing my bed-ridden relative again and being able to produce the answer to that challenge, but, whatever, I felt an inner push, a compulsion to keep on reading. There were only a couple more passages using the first day of the week. I might as well look at them. I had passed up my regular game of golf with the men in the ministerial association, so I decided to read on.

There are twenty-eight chapters in the book of Acts that tell about the actions of the apostles after Christ's resurrection. In the twentieth chapter there is an incident involving the first day of the week I wanted to investigate. I had already decided to pass over the verses dealing with the Sabbath because that was the Jewish holiday and had no bearing on the Christian's day.

In Acts 20:6–12 there is a story about Paul that most Bible scholars agree on in taking place around the year 57 A.D. That means that it occurred about 25 years after Christ returned to heaven. It goes like this: "And we sailed away from Philippi after the days of unleavened bread, and came unto them to Troas in five days; where we abode seven days." (It took 5 days for the group to travel from Philippi to Troas. Once there they stayed 7 days.) "And upon the first day of the week, when the disciples came together to break bread, Paul preached unto them, ready to depart on the morrow; and continued his

47

speech until midnight. And there were many lights in the upper chamber, where they were gathered together. And there sat in the window a certain young man named Eutychus, being fallen into a deep sleep, as Paul was long preaching, he sunk down with sleep, and fell down from the third loft, and was taken up dead. And Paul went down, and fell on him and embracing him, said, Trouble not yourself for his life is in him. When he (Paul) was come up again, and had broken bread, and eaten, and talked a long while, even till break of day, so he departed.'' The next verses say that Paul actually walked on to Assos, a trip of about 30 miles that same day! 30 miles!

Since I had just had that soul-shaking experience of thinking I had found the perfect text and having it turn out to be directly different from all I believed and had been taught, I did not get too excited at first. It looked like I had finally found it. But, I was not going to jump up and shout for joy until I had at least reread it one time. I reread it not once, but four times. Every time I read it it reinforced my beliefs. They were meeting Sunday night. Paul was preaching. They were holding communion, the Lord's supper, too. The believers were all together. It had to be the text. Nothing in it denied the fact that 25 years after Jesus returned to Heaven the disciples were observing Sunday in honor of His resurrection. Paul was leading out. It confirmed it all. The pressure lifted. I felt really relieved.

Through the years I have tried to keep a good library of books and all new translations of the Bible. There were several translations on the desk in front of me. I reached over and picked up one to read how another version described this Sunday evening worship service. It turned out to be the American Bible Society's version of the New Testament in Today's English Version. It was a paperback copy and had large letters reading ''Good News for Modern Man.'' I had just gotten good news from that passage in Acts and felt that this translation was just going to add to my well being.

When I turned to the twentieth chapter of Acts I saw

48

that an artist had made a little line drawing of the incident. There were smoking oil lanterns hanging from the ceiling. About 18 men and ladies were all in a circle, sitting and listening to one man. I gathered that the man standing with both hands raised was Paul. In the window was the slumping form of that sleeper. Then I read this under the picture: "On Saturday evening we gathered together for the fellowship meal."[1] "On Saturday evening?" "A fellowship meal?"

Now, how in the world could an organization as large as the American Bible Society make such a gross mistake? I wondered why they would say something like that.

The New English Bible puts it this way: "On the Saturday night, in our assembly for the breaking of bread, Paul, who was to leave the next day, addressed them,. . . ."[2]

I was forced to investigate some commentaries, dictionaries, and encyclopedias. I asked another minister that I had learned to respect for his knowledge of the Bible for his commentaries. And that time of perplexity and frustration proved to be more valuable than a college or seminary cram course.

Remember that the Bible counts time from sunset to sunset? Have you ever wondered why? In Genesis I discovered something that you probably already know. In the first chapter of Genesis is the story of the creation of the world. In several verses you find a certain statement repeated several times. In verse 5 it reads like this: "And God called the light Day, and the darkness He called Night." Then it adds this: "And the evening and the morning were the first day." Verse 8 says, "And the evening and the morning were the second day." Verse 13 says, "And the evening and the morning were the third day." And it is the same for each of the days of creation week. Do you know why "evening" was mentioned first? Sure, God started it all out in darkness, didn't He? In verse 2 you read this: "And the earth was without form and void, and darkness was upon the face of the deep." So, from the time the sun sets, at evening, until it sets again the next evening constitutes one whole day of 24 hours. I had to think it through like this:

The first day ends at sunset Sunday.

The second day ends at sunset Monday.

The third day ends at sunset Tuesday.

The fourth day ends at sunset Wednesday.

The fifth day ends at sunset Thursday.

The sixth day ends at sunset Friday.

The seventh day ends at sunset Saturday.

The Jews kept the seventh day Sabbath from sunset Friday to sunset Saturday. They started with the evening on Friday and continued on until the evening on Saturday.

The Bible recognizes a day from sunset to sunset, not from midnight to midnight. Everyone could know, without any watch or clock, when a day ended and the next one was to begin. All they had to do was to look at the setting sun.

I wondered, "How did we ever get to the place where we count time from the middle of the night to the middle of the next night?" Since the Bible said that the seventh day comes to an end at sunset, I realized that the first day of the week, according to the Bible, begins at sunset on Saturday.

The day we now call Sunday actually begins at sunset Saturday and ends at sunset on Sunday. Sure, the day ends with the setting of the sun!

I remembered when I was a building contractor before becoming a Christian, and I had to go and pick up a carpenter and take him to work every day. He lost his driver's license because he had imbibed too much in the spirits, the liquid kind. Every day as he left the house he would turn to his wife and say, "I'll see you when the sun sets, at the end of the day." Strange how things like that come back to you.

So, I figured it out! When the Bible said that Paul and the believers in Troas were meeting together at night on the first day of the week, it would have had to have been Saturday night, because the first day of the week began at sunset Saturday and continued on until sunset Sunday. The only dark period in that 24 hours would have been from Saturday evening to Sunday morning. So, it was not a church worship service on Sunday night after all. It was a farewell party for Paul who was going on to new mission fields. It was not a normal church worship service.

I was still bewildered over this because they were "together to break bread." That was a communion service. It is also called "The Lord's Supper." Man, I was puzzled.

A research with the term "breaking bread" revealed to me that it can be one of two things: it can be either the communion service or actual partaking in a meal.

In Acts 2:46 it tells of the early believers, "And they, continuing daily with one accord in the temple, and breaking bread from house to house did eat their meat with gladness and singleness of heart." So, which one was it in the case of Paul, the midnight meeting, and breaking bread?

Paul, himself, relates to us that he received a direct order from the Lord about properly conducting the communion service. The 11th. chapter of 1st. Corinthians is devoted to instructing us in the correct procedures. Quoting Jesus, he says, "As often as ye eat this bread, and drink this cup, ye do shew [show] the Lord's death till He come."

So, the Lord's Supper can be held anytime, not just on the Lord's day and at church. There is no set Biblical time or place. Paul and his believers were observing it when they got together to pay their parting respects.

Even though some might disagree with me, I sort of picture a very solem group of people in that third floor room. They loved Paul and hated to see him leave. After they had offered prayer, observed the communion service, and then sat back to listen to Paul tell of their need to be faithful to Christ. They were so engrossed in Paul's words that time meant nothing. Around midnight the man fell down to his death. After God had miraculously healed him through Paul, they all returned and took some refreshments out. They ate a light snack, and Paul talked on until around 6:00 A.M. They joined hands and united in prayer in behalf of this departing saint. Paul was a

51

missionary. He was traveling to various churches telling them, in long messages it seems, about the missionary work around the world. He was now going on to another assignment. He had been with the believers there seven days. He was saying good-bye. Probably some of the ladies had made some food and drinks for the occasion, as well as for Paul to munch on as he walked the entire next day. Maybe they took up a collection for Paul to use in his missionary efforts.

This was a hard pill to swallow. Yet, the truth was clearly seen. I thought again about that challenge, "Bill, I wish you would give me just one text to prove what you just said."

Strangely enough, I had just one text left! There was only one more time the New Testament uses the term "the first day of the week" and it was in a letter Paul wrote to the Christians in Corinth. The believers back in Jerusalem were having a real difficult time because of their faith in Christ. Thirty years after Jesus died for their sins Paul writes to the Corinthians and tells them that he wants them to do something for those persecuted Christians.

In I Corinthians 16:1–3 he tells them what he wants them to do: "Now concerning the collection for the saints, as I have given order to the churches of Galatia, even so do ye. Upon the first day of the week, let every one of you lay by him in store, as God has prospered him, that there be no gatherings when I come."

Had I been correct in using this text to encourage my members to come to church on Sunday and bring their offerings to place them in the collection plate?

Paul said he wanted these faithful members to help those other Christians and "let every one of you lay by him in store." That was the key. The New English Bible says, "Each of you is to put aside and keep by him a sum in proportion to his gains."

The Good News for Modern Man renders it this way, "Each of you is to put aside some money, in proportion to what he has earned, and save it up."

The New Testament In The Language of Today by William F. Beck is more specific: "Each of you should at home lay aside some money . . . and save it."[3]

Then the Weymouth Translation reads like this, "Let each of you put on one side and store up at his home whatever gain has been granted him."[4]

I did not have much difficulty in seeing how I had been wrong. There is no mention at all about the members coming to church on Sunday and placing their offerings in the collection plate. The Bible said, "Lay by him in store," and I had never, ever really read it.

Since Friday is the preparation day it is always a busy one. The men were working as long as they could on Friday, and, yet, not be so long as to prevent their being home, cleaned up, and ready for the family worship service at sundown. So, the natural time for them to figure out their gains and income was after the Sabbath had ended. The first day of the week was the most logical time.

Paul wanted someone of responsibility to go from home to home and put all the funds together. Paul would get it on his way to Jerusalem without having to call a special church meeting.

I had researched all the texts in the New Testament dealing with the first day of the week and found out that there was not the first one that commanded us to go to church on Sunday.

Yet, how come we all did? Surely we weren't all wrong? The Lord Jesus did rise from the dead on Sunday and we wanted to pay our tribute, praise and thanksgiving to Him! Where were the passages confirming all this?

Being forced into an examination of truth can be absolutely perplexing. You know something is in the Bible but not being able to find it really makes you feel frustrated. I knew Sunday was right and yet I just could not get any proof for it. That is, I could not find one text using the term "the Lord's day" or "the first day of the week" that stated that Sunday, or the first day, was to be observed by New Testament Christians. I thought about that calm, quiet and confident visitor and his challenge. Little did I know that at the very same time he had asked me to give him that one text there was a rancher in Colorado who was placing a daily ad in the newspaper offering $25,000 in cash to anyone who would present to him from the King James Bible one single text telling that the seventh day had been dropped as the Christian's day and replaced by Sunday, or that ordered men today to worship on the first day of the week. Do you think that visitor knew about that offer?

Maybe it was a trick. Maybe the change was made and the term "the first day of the week" was not even used. Sure, it had to be some other terminology! Why had I not realized that before? It had to be changed in honor of Christ's resurrection opposed to the old memorial of creation. And with this thought in mind I discovered some amazing things.

First, let me share something spectacular I discovered regarding creation. Maybe you already know this but I did not! It was such a surprise I just could hardly believe my own Bible.

Whenever you read in the Bible about "God," how do you know if it is God the Father, God the Son, or God the Holy Spirit? You see, many, many times the three-lettered word "G-O-D" is used and it doesn't say which One it is. You have to read lots of verses before it or afterwards, and you also have to compare other scriptures with it to determine the truth.

For example, the Bible says, "In the beginning God created the heaven and the earth." It does not say which One it is, does it? I have always pictured a kind, patient, loving, white-haired, bearded majestic man on a huge throne. Most people picture about the same concept.

In the book of John you can read a poetic statement about the One who created our planet. In John 1:1–3 John says this, "In the beginning was the Word, and the Word was with God, and the Word was God. The same was in the beginning with God. All things were made by Him, and without Him was not anything made that was made."

That is kind of confusing! But, when you look at the fourteenth verse in the same chapter you have an explosive explanation. It goes like this: "The Word was made flesh, and dwelt among us, and we beheld His glory, the glory as of the only begotten of the Father, full of grace and truth."

John is poetically speaking of Jesus as the "Word." So, when you reread those three verses and substitute the word "Jesus" for "Word," it comes out this way, "In the beginning was Jesus. And Jesus was with God, and Jesus is God. Jesus was in the beginning with God. All things were made by Him, and without Him was not anything made that was made."

How about that? I told you it would be explosive! This one passage says that Jesus made everything on, and in, earth, and earth itself! Looking through other passages dealing with creation I found that Paul had written a most amazing statement in Hebrews 1:1–2. He said, "God, who at sundry times and in divers manners spake in times past unto the fathers by the prophets, hath in these last days spoken unto us by his Son, whom He appointed heir of all things, by whom He also made the worlds."

If that was not enough to stun my senses, I also found this, in I Corinthians 10:1–4, "Moreover brethren, I would not that ye should be ignorant, how that all our fathers were under the cloud and all passed through the sea (the Red Sea), and were all baptized unto Moses in the cloud and in the sea; and did all eat the same spiritual meat, and did all drink the same spiritual drink; for they drank of that spiritual Rock (notice a capital "R") that followed them, and that Rock was Christ."

Some translators say something to the effect that they drank of "that spiritual rock," or "that Supernatural Rock," but they all say it was Christ!

You see, the One who led His people out of bondage in Egypt through Moses is the same One who spoke in thundertones from smoking Mount Sinai and repeated to them the same ten commandments He had given to our

55

first forefathers in person in the Garden of Eden over 2,000 years earlier, . . . The Lord Jesus Christ!

Not only that, I discovered that it was Christ who spoke with Abraham, Isaac, and Jacob! It was the Son of God Himself who communed with King David those many years ago!

Then it all came clear to me why Jesus had told the religious leaders in Jerusalem, "Before Abraham was, I am."

It became even more clear why Jesus said over and over again, "If you love Me keep My commandments." He gave them to Adam and Eve, and later thundered them down to Moses on Mount Sinai!

Now, here comes the most explosive explanation of it all. I had wondered so many times why the last book in the Bible, the book of Revelation, inserted one puzzling verse in it just after quoting Jesus. In Revelation 22:12–13, Jesus said this, "And, behold, I come quickly, and my reward is with Me, to give every man according as his work shall be. I am Alpha and Omega, the beginning and the end, the first and the last." I never realized the significance of that saying of Christ's, "The Alpha and Omega, the first and the last," before. Now it hit me! Jesus created the earth in the beginning and He will come again and bring the world as we know it now to an end!

I was amazed at how I never realized that this earth was a pet project of the Lord's. He created it. He nurtured it. He protected it! He came and lived in person in it! He died on it! He died for it! He is in heaven interceding with God for it! And He is going to come back to it one day soon!

No wonder He said that He was "Lord even of the sabbath." It was Jesus Christ who established the seventh-day sabbath in the beginning! It was Jesus who "rested" on the seventh day of creation week and, get this, it was Jesus who "rested" on the seventh day after dying for mankind! Now I understood why He is the "Alpha and the Omega."

Then, it became clear as to why John inserted that verse

in Revelation 22 after Jesus had spoken. It is verse 14 and it goes like this: "Blessed are they that do His commandments, that they may have right to the tree of life, and may enter in through the gates into the city."

The reason why that visitor challenged me to find one text in the New Testament where it says that the first day of the week is now to replace the seventh day and we are to worship on that day and keep it holy, is that there are no texts like that!

The reason that Colorado rancher offered $25,000 to anyone who would present to him Biblical statements from the King James Version of the Bible that tells us that New Testament Christians are now to observe Sunday, or the first day of the week, is that there are no such texts! As difficult as it was to admit, the reason why the seventh day Sabbath is the Lord's day is that He made it to start with. I could see why Paul said, in Hebrews 13:8, those famous words, "Jesus Christ, the same yesterday, and today, and forever."

Later studies revealed to me that I was not the first minister who was preaching on Sunday who discovered these soul-shaking revelations. Look at this: The founder of the Disciples of Christ, Alexander Campbell said this: "But, some say, the sabbath was changed from the seventh to the first day. Where? When? And by whom? No man can tell. No it was never changed! Nor could it be, unless creation was to be gone through again. For the reason assigned must be changed before the observance can be changed. It is old wives' fables to talk of the change of the seventh to the first day."[5]

The Toronto, Canada newspaper, The Albertan, October 27, 1949: "Philip Carrington, American Archbishop of Quebec, sent local clergymen into a huddle today by saying outright that there was nothing to support Sunday being kept holy. Carrington told a church meeting in this city of straight-laced Protestantism that tradition, not the Bible, had made Sunday the day of worship. He quoted the Biblical commandment which said "The seventh day is the sabbath, and said it should be the one of rest. He then stated that nowhere in the Bible is it laid down that worship should be done on Sunday. The Archbishop told a hushed, still audience. Local parsons read his comments today with set, determined looks. They refused to comment.''

James Cardinal Gibbons, Catholic scholar and writer, wrote in his famous book, Faith of Our Fathers: "You may read the Bible from Genesis to Revelation, and you will not find a single line authorizing the sanctification of Sunday.''[6]

I had to agree with him, against my will, because I had done exactly that. I had read the Bible from Genesis to Revelation trying to find that single line authorizing the sanctification of Sunday. And I just could not find the first single one! "Ah but the calendar has been changed," I thought to myself, "How do you know Saturday today is the same. Did the calendar make a change in the days of the week?''

Several answers. First, the Lord did not lose sight of the Sabbath. He would never have commanded us to do something that later was going to be impossible because of a man-made change. The Orthodox Jewish people have never had any question about it. They still recognize the seventh day as the Sabbath. Their records show an unbroken sequence since the days before Christ. They keep the sabbath day all across the world.

Second, the calendar did not change the weekly cycle. It takes 30 days for the moon to revolve around us. But, it takes 365 and ¼ days for us to revolve around the sun. We have added an extra day every four years to make up that one-fourth of a day. We call it "leap year." But, the "leap year" doesn't alter the regular weekly cycle. The calendar change simply made the world equal and uniform in its dating. The date of September 2 was moved up to September 14 to make this uniformity.

I wrote to the Royal Astronomer in London for help. I asked him three questions. First, is there any doubt that there is an unbroken sequence of the week as far as reliable records go? Second, did the calendar change, in any way, affect the weekly cycle so that one day might have been lost, passed over, or eliminated from its normal position? And then third, is today's Saturday the same as in the days of Christ?

Here is the Royal Astronomer's reply: "In reply to your letter of 15 October, I have to advise you that there is no reason to doubt the statement regarding the unbroken sequence of the week as far as reliable records go.

Secondly, it is certain that introduction of the Gregorian Calendar is 1582 and equally its introduction into the British Dominions in 1752 in no way affected the cycle of the week. Certain specific provision was made in the 1752 Act that although September 2 was immediately followed by September 14, these dates were successive days of the week, namely Wednesday and Thursday.

Thirdly, there is no reason to doubt that present day Saturdays are an exact number of weeks after the Saturday between the first Good Friday and Easter Sunday. Yours Faithfully, Harold W. Richards, For Astronomer Royal.

That about did it! The facts I did not want to face were right there before me. The Lord did definitely create a special day and set it aside as a holy day for man. That holy day is called the Sabbath in the Bible. The Sabbath is the seventh day of the week. So, then, since Saturday is the seventh day, Saturday is the Sabbath. According to the indisputable facts before me I had to honestly admit that the seventh day Sabbath and the Lord's day were one and the very same day! Saturday is the Lord's day! It sounded strange just saying it.

Thinking back on the things I had learned about Satan's scheme to cover up the correct character of God from man, and his plot to keep man from that right relationship with God, I wondered something that you might be wondering about now. Could it be possible, even though it seems absolutely impossible, that Satan has actually ingenuously "Christianized" some more pagan practices when it comes to man's keeping that sanctified, holy day? Doesn't the

Lord intend for us to honor His death, burial and resurrection by keeping the day He rose from the grave? If this is not the real way, then how do we celebrate those precious things? What does the Bible really say about sinful man praising and honoring his Saviour? I just had to know. And one more thing. Does it really matter which day you keep just as long as you sincerely and thankfully keep one day?

5/SO THAT'S HOW THEY DID IT!

The road is called "The Woodpecker Trail," and it goes from the bottom to the top of Florida, and then on upwards into the North. My family and I were driving on that road through the Everglades Swamp. Way down the road ahead of me I could see three large smokestacks. White smoke billowed out of the smokestacks and up into the air, disappearing into the clouds. I do not know why I stared at them. I guess it was just natural. But, just then, without any prior notice or warning, my smallest son, Jay, age five, jumped from the second seat of our three seater station wagon right up into the front next to me! It scared me half out of my wits as he pointed to the smokestacks, exclaiming, "So that's where they do it!"

When I had somewhat regained my composure I asked him, "So that's where they do what?"

And in that perfect childhood innocency he replied, "So that's where they make clouds!"

There were several things plaguing my mind when I discovered that there was no Biblical mention of a new day of worship. One of the most bewildering questions was, "If Christ did not intend for me to worship on another day other than the seventh-day Sabbath, how does He want me to honor His death, burial and resurrection?"

The second puzzling thing about it was, "If a change has really come into Christianity and sincere people are actually missing out on the real day of worship, who made this attempted change? How could it possibly not have been detected before? How could sincere Christians allow such a terrible violation to take place right before their very own eyes?'' It seemed impossible to do.

The third puzzle in all this was "Why did someone try to get Christians away from the true day?"

If there really was a mix-up, a covering over, or a deliberate attempt to throw Christians off the track, I wanted to know just how. In other words, just like my son, I wanted to be able to establish "So that's how they did it!"

But first, I had to establish one definite fact. Does the Lord want me to worship on another day, the first day of the week, in honor of his death, burial and resurrection? If not, then I would have to figure out how He really wants me to pay homage to His death, burial and resurrection.

In reading through the New Testament writings of the Apostle Paul, I found a lengthy letter he had written to the Christian believers in a place called Corinth. He repeats to them something he had apparently spoken directly to them when he was there in person. As he repeats the concern he makes sure that they understand that it is not his idea he is trying to get across to them.

In I Corinthians 11:23–26, he says this, "For I have received of the Lord that which also I delivered unto you (in person).''

Have you ever had any doubts when you have heard a minister claim that the Lord had spoken to him telling him to do certain things? Most of us wonder about these supposed conversations. Well, Paul makes it clear that he had actually heard directly from the throne about this particular concept. You see, when Paul was converted he did not get an opportunity to attend a Christian college, go to a highly respected seminary, take a correspondence course, or have a Bible worker come into his home and study the Bible with him. Paul went to Arabia and isolated himself from all outside human influences. He had just the section of the Bible available at that time, the Old Testament, and studied it in depth. He earnestly prayed for the Holy Spirit to lead him into a complete and true understanding of the Bible and the entire plan of salvation. So, he could honestly state that he had received all his information from the Lord because he had! What was it he had delivered to them earlier? He said it was this: "For I have received of the Lord that which also I delivered unto you, that the Lord Jesus Christ the same night in which He was betrayed took bread, and when He had given thanks, He brake it, and said, Take, eat; this is My body, which is broken for you. This do in remembrance of me." What do you call this particular ritual? Sure, it is the "Lord's Supper," or "Communion." Paul continues, "After the same manner also He took the cup, when He had supped, saying, This cup is the new testament in My blood; this do ye, as oft as ye drink it, in remembrance of Me! For as often as ye eat this bread and drink this cup, ye do show the Lord's death til He come."

How could I have missed this majestic meaning before? Sure, the Lord said it was the memorial of His death. The bread represents His body broken for me. The wine, or fruit juice, represents His shed blood. The Today's English Version made it even clearer, "For until the Lord comes, you proclaim His death whenever you eat this bread and drink from this cup."

Before the Lord died He did, indeed, talk about a change. He was going to wipe out the ceremonial laws that dealt with man making his trips to the tabernacle to cut the throat of a lamb, see the priest catch the blood of that innocent lamb, and the priest take the blood in before the Lord. It was all a symbol of the Lamb of God who would take away the sins of the world! Now, that was to be replaced by the communion service, the Lord's Supper. Sure, it all made sense. But, what about observing His resurrection on that great and glorious morning? Paul, once again, gives the answer. In Romans 6:3–5 I read this, "Know ye not, that so many of us as were baptized into Jesus Christ were baptized into His death? Therefore we are buried with Him by baptism into death; that like as Christ was raised up from the dead by the glory of the Father, even so we also should walk in newness of life. For if we have been planted together in the likeness of His death, we shall be also in the likeness of His resurrection.''

In reading the J. B. Phillips Translation I saw this, ''Have you forgotten that all of us who were baptized into Jesus Christ were, by that very action, sharing in His death?''[7]

That was a great and piercing revelation to me! For the first time in my entire ministry, and in the many times I had read the Bible, I could see the real significance of a person's being lowered into the water in complete immersion, and then, being raised up out of the water. Sure, it is a perfect picture presentation of the death, burial and resurrection of our Saviour!

Baptism by immersion is the beautiful memorial ceremony prescribed by the Lord for each individual who accepts His death, burial and resurrection in his or her behalf.

As I sat looking at the mental picture of a person walking into a creek, lake, river or a baptismal tank in a church, I could see the minister easing that person backwards into the water. I could see the face completely submerged under the water. And then the picture passed before me of several people I had baptized and the beautiful way in which they had came up out of that water completely relieved and revived! They all had expressions of joy, peace, and contentment.

Many denominations were not following this Biblical memorial! Lots of churches were using another form of ''baptism.'' How did there come a difference in the modes and methods of baptism? The word itself simply means ''to be immersed under.'' How was it that some of Christendom does not follow that divinely ordained method? I had to know.

My research took me back to the ancient practice of sun worship. The worshippers of the moon, stars and sun were very superstitious people. They worshipped tangible objects that could be seen. As time passed, the number of ''gods'' increased. Not too many years after the adulterous and idolatrous Queen Semiramis had gone to the grave in death, there came into being another god. This god, get this now, was like other gods of the sky. It was the god of rain.

This god of rain, the ancient sun worshippers were taught, got angry at the humans on earth one day and was so mad he wept. He wept and wept and wept until his tears flooded the earth. So, a pagan teaching came into existence, like all the others, to take man away from the truth concerning the Creator of heaven and earth. It was an attempt to conceal the truth from man about the Creator's flood.

So, in paganism being a demonstrative religion, a pagan ceremony was contrived whereby the new born baby was "protected" from being washed away in another crying spell of the god of rain. After a lot of wild and elaborate demonstrations of the priests that were supposed to capture the attention of the rain god, the prophet of Baal (Baal being the sun) would call for the mother and the father and the infant to come to a certain designated place. With lots of chanting and dancing around and over the baby, the priest dipped his hand into a container of water that had been dedicated to the rain god. He then sprinkled some of the water over the entire body of the baby. This sprinkling was thought to be a sort of immunity to, and an appeasement of, the rain god!

That ritual was handed down to man through ancient Babylon to Medo-Persia to Greece to Rome and on to Roman Catholicism and finally on into Protestantism just like all of the other segments of Lucifer's counterfeit Christian doctrines adopted by some of modern Christendom.

As I learned this amazing account of the mixture of sun worship into Christian baptism, I wondered, "What other things am I doing right now that are actually a watered-down blend of sun worship and Christianity? Am I doing anything else that is not one hundred percent Biblical?" But back to the plaguing puzzle before you.

The divinely approved method of celebrating the resurrection of Jesus Christ, it seems, is giving your heart and life to the One who died for you, accepting His death on the cross in your behalf, determining that you will live the Christian life as He gives you the power, and having the hope of eternal life with Him one day soon; and then, showing your acceptance of His death and resurrection in your behalf, you follow the Lord Jesus into the watery grave of baptism. When all this has sincerely been done, then you, according to the Bible, begin to walk that new life in Christ.

The New English Bible makes a strong point in the similarity of the believer being baptized by immersion and the actual death of Christ. It says, "Have you forgotten that when we are baptized into union with Christ Jesus we were baptized into His death? By baptism we were buried with Him, and lay dead, in order that, as Christ was raised from the dead in the splendour of the Father, so also we might set our feet upon the new path of life."

That is tremendous! Why did I have to learn these things the hard way? The swindle of all swindles was coming more and more into focus, and I was learning fantastic facts! But, there were lots of unanswered questions.

If the rituals and rites of the Lord's Supper, the Communion service, were the ones ordained by the Lord to celebrate His death; and if the beautiful service of baptism by immersion was the only heavenly instituted memorial of Christ's resurrection, how did Sunday come to be such a widely accepted substitute?

In the early centuries after Christ's sojourn in visible form on earth, Lucifer launched an all-out campaign to conquer the infant church of Christ. In every conceivable, and inconceivable, fashion, at every point, sun worship invaded Christendom. It was not long after the Christian church began establishing a strong missionary outreach into all the then-known world that Lucifer's own outreach came right in behind. Within 200 years there was such an invasion of pagan sun worshipping teachings into Christendom that the true gospel message was twisted and warped! It became a combination of the truth and mystical, mythical, superstitious rites, ceremonies, and teachings in many of the churches and among most believers.

The highlight of sun worshipping activities centered around the day called Sun-day. The day of the sun became the day of sin. On that day the sun worshippers observed very immoral and lewd ceremonies that would not even pass X-rated censors today! All was done in the honor of the sun. All done on one special day, the Sun-day.

The high day of the true Christians was the Sabbath, the seventh day! On that day the followers of the Man from Galilee met together in reverent and happy harmony. Prayers of thanksgiving, songs of praise, and the ministry of the Word took place among the groups of faithful, loving Christians. All done in the honor of the Son!

Every week there were two different groups of people carrying on religious services. Every week there were two different days being observed. The Sabbath and the Sun-day.

In the first part of the fourth century the Romans ruled the world. The Roman Empire was ruled by a man named Constantine. This Roman Emperor was a sun worshipper. Constantine was a Roman sun-worshipping emperor who got into trouble. The Roman people were becoming dissatisfied, and wanted a change. The emperor heard all the rumors and rumblings. He had to do something to solidify his empire. He became a shrewd politician. He attempted to make everyone in the realm happy and contented. You know the old story, "a car in every garage and a chicken in every yard." But, sometimes things are easier said than done!

He made a royal decree that he felt would make most of his realm happy. He announced that the Sun-day was to become a legal holiday! Now the governmental offices closed and shops shut their doors on the first day of the week, the Sun-day. Most work ceased on the venerable day of the sun. It was a smart move. The people soon forgot their dissatisfaction. The Sun-day closing law was a successful decreee! However, also in his realm was a fast-growing organization called Christianity. This Sun-day law also affected them. He began consultations with the rulers of the church of Rome. And it was not long before Constantine performed another political precedent. Constantine accepted the invitation to become a member of the church! Now, through this move, it was thought that all factions within the realm would be eliminated and peace would prevail.

But instead of a blessing it proved to be a real Pandora's box that opened up many conflicts and confrontations. You see, the church at Rome had also departed somewhat from the original Biblical teachings. Not too much, but just enough to embrace a number of sun-worshipping teachings to make it on very uneasy grounds. When the Emperor became a member of the church, if only in name alone, it was an opportunity of a lifetime! Now maybe these millions and millions of pagans could be brought to Christ! And the church of Rome began wooing and winning the sun worshippers to this new way of life. With Constantine as the chief example, many, many sun worshippers became church members. The church saw a sharp rise in membership. The church was growing. But, the plan was to backfire!

Many ministers will admit today that not every member in their churches is genuinely converted. It was true in the case of the sun worshippers uniting with the church. Only it was the exception, and not the rule, when a sun worshipper was genuinely converted to Christ. And as the membership list continued to place more and more of these unconverted pagans to it, the sooner the plan would backfire.

It has not been too long since the ten million member Methodist Church met in Texas with the much, much smaller United Brethren Church for the purpose of consolidating both groups into one. Guess which one of the two groups had to do most of the compromising in the merger? Sure, the name of the consolidated church tells the story. It was not the Brethren-Methodist, or the United Brethern, but, instead the United Methodist Church. So, the smaller of the two groups made more concessions.

The very same thing happened to the church of Rome. When the membership grew to the place where there were many, many more unconverted sun worshippers than Christians, then the majority began to rule. It was this leading pagan, sun-worshipping majority within the church that caused the church, through the years, to accept and adopt more and more sun worshipping teachings and practices, and to "Christianize" them.

The majority elected the officers and leaders. Within the period of a little less than two hundred years after Constantine had made his nominal profession of Christianity the vast majority of governmental officers within the church were sun worshippers, And instead of converting the sun worshippers, the church was converted to paganism. Slowly more and more Biblical teachings were united with sun worship, and sun worship united with Christianity. And it was not much longer after that before the church was Christian in name only.

The most outstanding replacement was that of the Sabbath. The venerable day of the Sun was observed by the largest percentage of the church people even in the early stages of the church following the emperor's admission into the church. And within a few years there were so very few Christians within the church observing the true Lord's day that the change was made with hardly a murmur or complaint.

I wondered how in the world those true Christians, who really loved the Lord, could sit back and let such a blasphemous change take place. Why did they just do nothing?

When you realize that for over 200 years both the Sabbath and the Sun-day were observed each and every week, and when you realize that these special events each had different meanings, and when you realize that the majority observed the Sun-day, it is easy to see how a gradual change could take place.

One more thing. Since a new generation comes along on the average of every 25 years, it meant that every 25 years a new generation came into existence where the Sun-day was stressed by an ever-growing majority. With Christianity being stressed less and less with each new generation, it did not take too many generations before Christendom was almost a forgotten word in Rome.

So, plain and simple, the majority made the change after a long period of gear shifting.

Before you start to criticize the average church member for letting that change take place, remember something. Remember that there were no gigantic printing presses all over the realm rolling off tremendous numbers of copies of the Bible every day. The average member never, ever saw a Bible, much less read it for himself.

Religious leaders told the lay people what the Bible was supposed to teach. And with most of the religious leaders within the church following a watered-down blend and mixture of satanic teachings and Christian doctrines they, themselves, did not really know what the Bible actually taught. Each successive generation of religious leaders was gradually being taken away from the Bible and into paganism with a Christian name. So, very, very few knew enough about the Bible to know that the change was not a Biblical one after all.

But, Satan is still a very shrewd manipulator. He covered his tracks in this change so hardly any future generations would ever find them. Since the first day of the week is the day that Christ did rise from the grave, the change was all passed over under the theory that it was to be a tribute to Christ's resurrection. Since Christ rose on the venerable day of the Sun, it was a tribute to both the Sun and the Son!

The years passed. So did a knowledge of the Bible. Except for a few isolated groups here and there, hardly anyone knew anything about the plan of salvation in the

Bible. It became "The Dark Ages." God is patient but determined! God finally intervened to bring back His erring people. Martin Luther was one of the first leaders through whom the Lord was to lead His people back to a right relationship with him. You know the story. Through his personal study of the Bible, disapproved in his day, and through the conviction of the Holy Spirit, Luther came to a knowledge of some of the errors in the church's teachings. He tried to bring the church around to the proper study of, and the right teachings of, the Bible. But, as you know, the church would not accept his counsel. He did not want to start a new church. Nevertheless, Martin Luther started his people back on the route to the kingdom of heaven. As dedicated and devoted as Luther was, however, he did not return to all of the segments of Christianity.

The Lord, in His omniscience, knew that it was too much of a giant step for these people to take. They had to be led back to all of the teachings of the Bible, step by step, generation after generation. Slowly and deliberately did the Lord lead His people. Truth after truth after truth.

Now, in these closing days of time, the Lord is leading His people to the understanding, and acceptance, of all of Christian truth. One of the things He is leading men, women, and young people to is the knowledge of the invasion of these sun-worshipping theories, practices, and the rejection of them all.

I wondered at the way He had led me to understand some of these things. Things I never even thought about before. Too bad I had to have so many problems, failures, and backslidings before I received this new insight. I sure am sorry that I disappointed Him so much. But, the Lord is leading men, women, and young people all across the entire earth to the thrilling discovery of the long-lost doctrine of the Lord's day. Every day, across the world, people who never ever realized there was any question over what day the true Christian would keep in honor of His resurrected Lord, are learning of the true Biblical day!

My investigation of these people, and my conversations

71

with them, prove that they are finding those promises of God to bless His people for their faithful, loving obedience are more bountiful and blessed than they ever believed.

Does it really make any difference what day you keep just as long as you keep one day? A special wedding might give you the answer. Let me tell you about it.

This special wedding was conducted by the bride's father and the groom's father. Both men jointly officiated. It was held in a church in Massachusetts. It was special because the groom was my son, Steve. Steve met Beverly almost five years before. A lovelier wedding scene I have never witnessed. Everyone sensed a special bond between these two that is seldom seen today. For five long years Steve and Beverly had waited for this day. After the wedding there was a beautiful reception. Everyone knew full well that these two Christian young people were being joined together by God. It was indeed a solemn and joyous occasion, at the same time.

Steve and Beverly finally were able to break away from the large crowd of well-wishers and leave on their long-anticipated honeymoon. They say that it was more delightful and fulfilling than either had dreamed.

Now, what would you say, if sometime later, the bride's father, along with his other daughter, Renita, came out to see Steve. The father-in-law tells Steve that there is going to be a change. "I want you to take Renita as your wife instead of Beverly. It is all right. Don't worry about it. It really doesn't matter that much which daughter you marry just as long as you marry one. I will authorize the change." Of course this did not happen. But what do you think Steve would do? You know what you would do. You would not stand for any such change, would you? You married that one girl and you want that same one. God instituted the Sabbath and Marriage in the Garden of Eden. They are sacred. The Lord has never changed the seventh day Sabbath to the first, or any other day. He wants to keep the original one.

With this new-found discovery of the Lord's special and

holy day being the very same one He gave to mankind at the creation of this world, the seventh day, I set out to share it with other ministers who I thought would be delighted to hear the news. But, to my sudden surprise, not everyone shared my enthusiasm!

6/A MAN, MOUNTAIN, AND MESSAGES

I am sure that you have heard the much-repeated statement that "Zeal without knowledge is dangerous." Well, it also is very, very embarrassing!

The very first fellow minister I shared my recent discovery with was a man that I had traveled to certain speaking engagements with, and one I considered a real friend. My excitement caused him to sit and listen intently as I gave a short summary of the Lord's day and the Sabbath being one and the very same day. His attentiveness to my enthusiastic giving of this good news was a thrill. Someone else, now, was going to rejoice in a rich discovery! At least, that was what I was getting from his silence. Before I had really gotten into the Biblical findings that really proved all this, he sat up out of his seat, interrupted me kindly, and said, "Man, don't you know about Romans 6:14?"

"Bill," he smiled very understandingly, "We're not under those old laws any more, we are free! We are under grace." And he began to quote several passages that sounded like New Testament Christians were "liberated" from the old harsh laws God gave to just the Jewish people.

Before I could ask a few questions he "had to leave to keep an important appointment." But, as he departed he gave one parting shot, "Remember, read Romans 6:14."

I immediately went for the first Bible I could find to see what Romans 6:14 did say. Paul wrote the book of Romans, and in that verse he said, "For sin shall not have dominion over you, for ye are not under the law, but under grace." Sure, I knew that verse, but I didn't remember it when he said it. He said that this verse proves that we do not have to keep the fourth commandment now.

There were some other verses he quoted. Reading through most of the New Testament I found them. There was this one from Galatians 3:24, that said, "Wherefore the law was our schoolmaster to bring us unto Christ . . ." He had fervently used this one to let me know that the Sabbath commandment, the fourth one in God's ten commandments, was no longer needed since Jesus had come. It pointed us to the Lord and since the Lord has come, it was not in effect any more.

The other text he really stressed I found in Colossians 2:14, and it read, "Blotting out the handwriting of ordinances that was against us, which was contrary to us, and took it out of the way, nailing it to his cross." "Jesus nailed those old laws to His cross, Bill; didn't you know that?" No, I didn't know that. After I had left him I had a big lump in my throat. I knew that I had made a serious mistake spending so much time trying to develop what I considered "good sermons" and all the time I should have been studying into things like this. I determined to know the truth.

That short session with my minister friend made me burn the midnight oil for many moons! There was only one way to solve this issue once and for all. I had to go back to the Bible and read what it said about the "law," and its relationship to all of us today.

Let me tell you something. This study did not begin because of a wounded pride. I had lots of work to do. The pressure of two sermons each Sunday was very much there. There was also that long list of visitations that took time itself. I was not overlooking that mid-week service that demanded lots of preparation, too. My family had needs as well as the church. Several appointments and meetings were also scheduled! But, there was an inner turmoil, an unrest, that drove me on to find out the truth regardless of how long it took. I know now where that pushing was coming from!

That push to know the truth gave me some astounding insights that I probably never, ever would have been privileged to encounter had I continued on in my using the Bible just to provide sermons.

Moses was commissioned to lead the Israelite nation out of slavery in Egypt. Their 400-year stay in that foreign land was now over. The Lord's basic training program for the Hebrews was completed. Now He wants to take them to a tax-free inheritance in a beautiful land where He will make them the most happy, healthy, humble, and holy people on the face of the globe. With the world looking on in absolute amazement at these most outstanding and successful people, the Hebrews were to teach the world about the true God. They were to be a special people with a special purpose.

Three months after they had marched out of Egypt nearly three million strong, they came to a 6,791-foot high mountain called Sinai, and also Mt. Horeb. Since their 400-year imprisonment was in the heart of pagan sun worship, the Lord has to do a spiritual deprograming!

Since the pagans used a great deal of display, color, noise, and emotion in their ceremonies that excited the imagination, the Lord uses a little visual aid of His own. He wants to impress the people with the sacredness of the occasion.

This is the way the Bible describes it in Exodus 19:16–19: "And it came to pass on the third day (third day after getting to Mount Sinai) in the morning that there were thunders and lightnings, and a thick cloud upon the mount, and the voice of the trumpet exceeding loud; so that all the people that were in the camp trembled. (They got the message. . . .they recognized something monumental and supernatural was taking place.) And Moses brought forth the people out of the camp to meet with God; and they stood at the nether (or lower) part of the mount. And

Mount Sinai was altogether on a smoke, because the Lord descended upon it in fire! And the smoke thereof ascended as the smoke of a furnace! And the whole mount quaked (shook) greatly! And when the voice of the trumpet sounded long, and waxed louder and louder, Moses spake, and God answered him by a voice.'' Then it happened! Verse 20 records: ''And the Lord came down upon Mount Sinai, on the top of the mount! And the Lord called Moses up to the top of the mount; and Moses went up.''

Moses hikes up to the top and God meets him there. The Lord gives Moses ten moral codes called ''The Ten Commandments.'' All ten of them are listed in Exodus chapter twenty and the first sixteen verses. For brevity's sake look at just a few of them: verse 3, ''Thou shalt have no other gods before me; verse 7, ''Thou shalt not take the name of the Lord thy God in vain''; verse 8, ''Remember the sabbath day to keep it holy.'' These Ten Commandments Moses received that day are known as ''The Moral Law.''

The Lord goes over these with Moses, and Moses goes back down among the people. Verse 20 records the next event: ''And Moses said unto the people, Fear not, for God is come to prove (or test) you, that His fear (or reverence for Him) may be before your faces, that ye sin not.'' Moses calms their fears by explaining that the Lord is simply laying out in simple terms the guideline that will give them peace, happiness and holiness. It is for their benefit and by it they will be blessed. I was amazed by the things happening next.

Verse 21 reads this way: ''And the people stood afar off and Moses drew near unto the thick darkness where God was!'' Moses makes a second trip back up those six thousand feet!

It was a surprise to realize that Moses made more than one hike up Mount Sinai. Most of us have been told about that one trip when he got the Ten Commandments. Now the Bible says he actually makes a second journey into the presence of God atop that dark, cloud-covered peak. Naturally, there has got to be a very important reason for the Lord asking Moses to walk another one and a quarter miles up that steep incline. The purpose is recorded in chapter 21. Again, for brevity's sake, a few example verses. God speaks in verses 1–2: "Now these are the judgments which thou shalt set before them; If thou buy an Hebrew servant, six years shall he serve; and in the seventh, he shall go out free for nothing."

Verses 18-19: "And if men strive together, and one smite another with a stone, or with his fist, and he die not, but keepeth (or is confined to) his bed, if he rise again and walk about upon his staff, then he that smote him shall be quit (free and clear), only he shall pay for the loss of his time (unemployment compensation), and shall cause him to be thoroughly healed (pay all medical bills)."

Verses 33–34: "And if a man shall open a pit, or if a man dig a pit, and not cover it, and an ox or an ass fall therein, the owner of the pit shall make it good, and shall give money unto the owner of them; and the dead beast shall be his (shall belong to the one who paid off).

These three examples are typical of all the regulations the Lord gave to Moses, and are found in chapters 21–24. They constitute what is called "The Civil Law." The Civil Law is God's instruction to His people for their dealings with each other. And, amazingly enough, you can trace practically all of our present day laws right back to these basic civil laws. In a nutshell, they are simply Christian community courtesies.

Moses made two trips up Mount Sinai and got two laws. Now, look at what happens next. Exodus 24:18 records this: "And Moses went up into the midst of the cloud, and gat him up into the mountain; and Moses was in the mount forty days and forty nights."

He made a third trip! This third trip saw him receiving the complicated "Ceremonial Law." Moses got detailed instructions about building the traveling tabernacle, the mobile church, and what the furnishings were to be. He also got the complicated directions for carrying on the services in, and around it. These instructions and directions were so complicated and detailed that it took Moses forty days to grasp it all! It also took the rest of the book of Exodus, all of Leviticus, and part of Numbers to record them all.

The Ceremonial Law pointed forward to the Lamb of God who would one day be offered as a sacrifice for our sins. Every time the priest carried out the ritual of the repentant sinner coming to the courtyard of the tabernacle, slicing the throat of the innocent sacrificial lamb, the priest catching some of the blood and taking it into the tabernacle to place on the horns of the altar, and then burning the carcass, the priest was supposed to instruct the sinner that this was a symbol of the real Lamb of God . . . the Messiah . . . the Saviour . . . the Lord Jesus Christ! The Ceremonial Law dealt with the ceremonies that portrayed the death of Christ for mankind's sins. Three trips up the mountain, three sets of laws!

Now, while Moses was in the mountain this third time receiving the Ceremonial Law, things began to happen back down in the valley! You know the story. The people grew fearful that something had happened to Moses. Forty days and no Moses! So they had begun a building project before the 40 days were even up. They started erecting a statue of a calf similar to the sun worshipper's god, Apis.

While they were building their idol, Moses was getting the intricate details about the Ceremonial Law worked out in his mind. God did not let Moses get distracted from his deep study. When Moses finally had the entire building program worked out in his mind, the comprehension of the furniture and fixtures clear, and understood, step by step, the rituals and their important significances, the Lord gave him one of the most amazing gifts! An intricate work of art!

Exodus 31:18 tells about this most unusual presentation: "And He gave unto Moses, when He had made an end of communing with him upon Mount Sinai, two tables of testimony, tables of stone, written with the finger of God!" How about that? Two large stone slabs with the Ten

Commandments engraved in them! And, think about it, the Lord actually struck stone before the trembling Hebrew leader, and in a moment, chiseled in the Hebrew language the very same Ten Commandments He spoke directly to Adam and Eve 2,400 years earlier! "Written with the finger of God!" Moses took them down to show them to his people.

When Moses saw what the people had done he was so angry at them that he threw the two stone slabs containing the miraculous engraving of the Ten Commandments all the way down from the high ledge he was on. They hit the valley's floor with loud thuds! They broke into pieces. The people became terrified and felt they were all going to be struck dead any moment. But as you know, God forgave them. Moses led them into a deep, repentant time of confession and, afterwards, appreciation and thanksgiving, and then, Moses had to have two new slabs chiseled out by the Hebrew people themselves. Moses then took the two man-made slabs all the way back up into the top of the mountain again, where God repeated the miraculous engraving on those two slabs.

It took a lot of hard labor to make the same size and thickness. It was hard on Moses to have to carry them, one under each arm, 6,791 feet up a mountain. But, isn't that the way it usually is; we make it so doubly hard for ourselves when we don't follow the instructions of the Infinite?

Now, just before the Israelites take off from Mount Sinai, heading for their new land, the Lord gives Moses one more set of instructions for the people. It is recorded in Deuteronomy, chapter 14 and also in Leviticus, chapter 11. Look at the way it is in a few example verses.

Leviticus 11:1–2: "And the Lord spake unto Moses and Aaron, saying to them, speak unto the children of Israel saying, These are the beasts (or animals) which ye shall eat among the beasts that are upon the earth."

Verse 9: "These ye shall eat of all that are in the waters."

Verse 13: "These are they which ye shall have in abomination among the fowls."

Verse 21: "Yet these ye may eat of every flying creeping thing that goeth about upon all fours, which have legs above their feet, to leap withal upon the earth."

What are these verses that I have been quickly skimming over saying? In verses 46–47, is the summary and explanation of both the eleventh chapter of Leviticus and the fourteenth chapter of Deuteronomy: "This is the law of the beasts, and of the fowl, and of every living creature that moveth in the waters, and of every creature that creepeth upon the earth, to make a difference between the unclean and the clean, between the beast that may be eaten, and the beast that may not be eaten." This last set of regulations dictated to Moses by the Lord is called "The Dietary Law." The Dietary Law simply spells out what are clean and what are unclean animals. It is the Lord's directions for what the proper diet was to be.

Now we come to the importance of mighty Moses and his many hikes up the mountain. It is very, very vital that it make an indelible impression. Moses was given four specific laws! God gave four different laws! They were the Moral, Civil, Ceremonial, and Dietary Laws. Four very specific regulations! All originating with the Creator!

Throughout the Bible these laws are spoken of as simply "the law." A few times they are referred to as the "Law of Moses." Please mark this well in your mind; the Hebrew people knew which law the prophet was talking about or the author was writing about. No one had to spell out the "Moral Law", or the "Civil Law", or the "Ceremonial Law", or the "Dietary Law". It was not necessary.

The Spanish language is a language of honesty! The language assumes that all of its users are honest. For example, it will say, "I put my hand into the pocket." In English we say, "I put my hand into my pocket." The spanish assume you would never be putting your hand into someone else's pocket!

The Hebrew language is an "understood" language,

81

also, it takes a lot for granted. It supposes that you "understand" many things and therefore does not spell out every little detail. So, the Bible writers in the Old Testament spoke of "the law" and they knew that the reader knew which one was being discussed. The New Testament writers, many of whom were Hebrew themselves, also followed the same pattern. The Greek writers did the same. So, for brevity's sake, as well as the "understood" concept, the Bible speaks of the "law" and the reader is supposed to determine if it is the "Moral", "Civil", "Ceremonial", or "Dietary".

But please, mark this well. The Bible makes it perfectly clear that God gave mankind, through the Hebrew leader Moses, four separate and distinct laws during that one year stay at Mount Sinai's valley. The reason the Bible records the many trips of that old patriarch up that mountain is to not only clarify a crucial mistake and misunderstanding making its mark among the Christian ministry and laity alike, but to show one of the ways Satan has cast a stupifying insensibility over spiritual leaders. That spell has set up the machinery to help accomplish Satan's fraud, hoax, and swindle. And I have to confess that through ignorance, and the lack of deep study into this ingenious scheme, I have been an unwitting accomplice.

When we ministers claim that New Testament Christians are no longer obligated to observe the fourth commandment because we are "not under the law, but under grace", could we be making a serious mistake with far-reaching consequences?

If we teach that the fourth commandment has been done away with, are we possibly misunderstanding and misinterpreting, the Master's message for mankind?

Are we correct when we read such Biblical statements about the law being a "schoolmaster" that was to teach us about Christ, and that once He came and brought about His completed plan of salvation, that schoolmaster has been eliminated?

Could there be some error in interpreting a passage of

Scripture about Christ nailing ordinances to His cross so it sounds like the fourth commandment was destroyed at the time of His death?

In looking at the term "law" in the New Testament, I did find a number of verses that really sounded like Paul and others were saying that the law has definitely been wiped away, destroyed, or done away with. And, of course, if the law has been eliminated, so would the fourth commandment dealing with the sanctity of the seventh-day Sabbath.

But, were these passages only "sounding like" they taught that? In I John 3:4 it says: "Whosoever committeth sin transgresseth also the law; for sin is the transgression of the law."

The Today's English Version renders that verse this way: "Whosoever sins is guilty of breaking God's law; because sin is breaking of the law."

The New English Bible says simply: "Whosoever sins breaks God's law."

Sin, is, in fact, "lawlessness."

Is the Bible contradicting itself? Are the skeptics correct in their charges of Biblical errors?

Paul sounds like he is teaching no more commandments, and John appears to believe they are still in effect. Since "sin is breaking of the law", how can we sin and not break God's Commandments?

You can ask the average minister, "Is it all right to kill?"

He will reply that it most definitely is not! He will generally say that God forbade those things in the ten commandments.

Go back and ask the same minister, "Should we keep the seventh day Sabbath according to the fourth commandment?"

He will immediately, and without hesitation, tell you that you do not have to keep the Sabbath because that commandment has been done away with!

Through the years I had heard the same explanation about the ten commandments repeated a number of times.

It always went right over my head. That explanation went something like this: "The Ten Commandments give us an insight to the personality and character of God." Now that is a little heavy! We have lots of theological terms that I am afraid sail over too many people's heads too often. We ministers like to use those descriptive phrases a lot. And the more intellectual it sounds the more often we use it. But, what does that description of God's Ten Commandments mean: "The Ten Commandments give us an insight to the personality and character of God"?

In my research I was brought to this realization: The Constitution of the United States of America reflects the personality and character of Americans. Any law reflects the people who made it. America was established because certain Christians wanted to live and work where they could have religious liberty. And the laws those Christians made are supposed to guarantee religious freedom for all. These sincere founding fathers made these laws because they felt they were best for the people. The U. S. Constitution reflects the views and goals of the early Americans for all Americans for all time.

So, by the same token, the Ten Commandment, moral law reflects the views and goals of God the Creator for all His creatures for all time! We know what the Creator is like by the laws He made for mankind. Now you see what the age-old definition of God's Ten Commandments means by giving us an insight to the personality and character of the Creator.

Not only did my research give me that insight, but I also discovered that practically all of Christendom agrees on the fact that the Ten Commandments can be divided into two basic themes. First, man's relationship with God. And, second, man's relationship with man. Actually the Ten Commandments really show us the secret for successful living! You see, when we truly follow the Lord's teachings and are right with God and our fellow man, then we are really happy and successful!

And the strange paradox in all this is that Christendom

agrees on this basic concept, and at the same time, continues on in its refusal to even listen to any suggestions that the Ten Commandments might be still in effect today. That is, the fourth one of the ten!

Malachi 3:6 tells us that the Lord said, "I change not!"

So, if the Ten Commandments are the eternal reflection of an unchanging God, how can they ever change? How can one of them be destroyed? How can one of them be altered if they are eternal?

The answer to all this is found back in those many mountain hikes of mighty old Moses. Remember that Moses made those trips up and down the mountain to pass on, not one, but many, messages from God for mankind.

When the Israelite nation, God's chosen people, left Mount Sinai, they left with four different and distinct laws for mankind. They were, again, the "Moral", the "Civil", the "Ceremonial", and the "Dietary" laws. And, here is the whole answer to the problem. One of those four laws and regulations came to an end when Jesus died! Only one was no longer needed after Christ's death for man became a reality!

Which law, or regulation, was it?

Was it the "Moral" law, the Ten Commandments? Now that Jesus has paid the penalty for your sins, are you free to commit adultery, murder, or covetousness? Of course not!

Now that Christ has died for your life, is the "Civil" law not to be carried out today? Is it correct to go out and treat your neighbor the way a criminal, thief, or rapist would? Are you to ignore his property and privacy? Naturally not!

Now that the Messiah's prophecies have been fulfilled and He completed His atoning sacrifice for you, has your responsibility to maintain a clean, healthy, and wholesome body and mind ceased? Is the "Dietary" law, condemning certain harmful foods, no more any good? No! Even the New Testament writers say our body doesn't even belong to us any more when we come to Jesus. We are told that we are under a deeper obligation to keep our bodies in good condition.

Okay, then, there is the "Ceremonial" law left. Is this the one that was to come to an end when Calvary's cross contained our Christ? When the true Lamb of God was slain, was the other necessary any more? When Christ shed His blood for you, was there any need for the innocent lambs to be led into the place of their shedding their blood as a symbol? No, the symbol was no more needed. The real Lamb of God had come! This ritual was the thing to be dropped. This blood-soaked service was to come to an end! The "Ceremonial" law was now outdated! You see, the "law" that pointed forward to Christ's sacrifice was the "Ceremonial" law. The "law" that was the "school-master" to teach us, and bring us to Christ was the "Ceremonial" law. The "law" that was "the handwriting of ordinances that was against us, that was contrary to us" was the rites and rituals of the "Ceremonial" law. Nothing was more "against us" and "contrary to us" than slitting a lamb's throat with a razor-sharp knife, and using that shed blood as a symbol of Christ's shed blood. That was the "law" that Jesus took and nailed to His cross!

So, whenever I read the Bible now I have learned to use the common sense that was expected of the people of old. I have to decide which "law" the writer is talking about when he uses that word "law." I have to think about it, for a second or two, and determine if it is the "Moral" or "Civil" law. I have to see the verses before it and figure out simply if it is the "Dietary" or the "Ceremonial" law. And it is not hard at all. It is very simple.

There is no contradiction at all in the Bible writers. We just have to use the "understood" method like our good Spanish friends. Do it, now, yourself, and see how easy it is.

Remember the stunning statement of Paul's in Romans 6:14, "For sin shall not have dominion over you, for ye are not under the law, but under grace."

Reread it, and put in the correct law. You will find it

86

goes like this, "For sin shall not have dominion over you, for ye are not under the (Ceremonial) law but under grace." How about that?

By the way, the word "grace" means: "unmerited favor," "undeserved gift," and "an unearned blessing." Think about it, that is exactly what God gave you when He gave His Son on the cross! He gave you an extra special favor you did not deserve, a fantastic and generous gift you did not merit, and a bountiful blessing you surely did not earn!

So, Paul is simply saying now that we have received that favor, gift, and blessing, can we take it all for granted and go on and sin? Paul was such a conscientious Christian that he tried to never, ever do the smallest, most insignificant, act if he thought it would cause some believer in Christ to sin. Surely he would not have encouraged a whole church to break the law of God!

As a matter of fact, in the verse that follows that much-misunderstood verse he actually said that we should not break the moral law of God. In Romans 6:15, Paul said, "What then, shall we sin, because we are not under the (Ceremonial) law, but under grace? God forbid!"

Since the ceremonies and rituals with lambs, the blood, the innocent animal deaths and all that, have been eliminated, can we take all this liberty and freedom for granted? Paul says, "No way! We are deeper in our obligations to not sin." Like God, His commandments are eternal.

Also, Paul wants us to realize that we are "not under the law" as a means of obtaining our salvation.

And another fact Paul emphasizes over and over again is that we are "not under the law" as far as its condemnation is concerned . . . that is, when Christ has saved us.

Now think about this puzzling dilemma. How does it happen, with all these facts before the entire Christian ministry for every single one to discover through prayer and deep study, that the largest majority still reject the Ten Commandments as the eternal principles and character of God the Creator? Why does Christianity, as a general rule, turn a deaf ear to even considering the validity of the fourth commandment?

Sometime ago in a certain Pennsylvanian city a little over 100 birds were found one morning lying dead at the base of the statue of William Penn. What caused their mysterious death? It seems that the night before there was a heavy fog. In the darkness and the fog these birds were flying south, and they struck the statue. They were flying too low!

What is the supernatural, benumbing spiritual power that is infiltrating the present-day Christian leadership and causing this completely mysterious and bewildering attitude of indifference? What is behind the strange apathy found in the largest percentage of clergymen today? What invisible power is blinding countless thousands of otherwise intelligent and sensible spiritual directors and causing them to be flying too low?

Could it be that the same one who has so silently and successfully slipped his satanic counterfeit teachings into Christianity is also brilliantly masterminding the most comprehensive assault against the Creator and Sustainer of this planet earth?

Are you seeing the foundation being laid for the supreme swindle of all swindles?

7/DREAMS, DREAMS, DREAMS

I think it was Josh Billings, the American comical writer, who said, "Don't ever prophesy. If you prophesy wrong, no one will forget it. If you prophesy right, no one will remember it."

In order to prevent you from falling victim to the satanic influx of pagan teachings into Christianity, the Lord gave you some advance warnings. This was done in what is known as "prophecy."

"History" means an account of past acts while "prophecy" means an account of future acts. It is God looking down the corridors of time and revealing some of it to you.

In the book of Daniel the Lord unfolds future acts in two dreams to two men. One man could not remember it. The other man could not forget it.

Many years passed after Nimrod and Semiramis fostered Lucifer's deceptive counterfeit, and the Jewish nation came into existence. They were to be such a happy, healthy, and holy nation that the rest of the world would not only be amazed at them, but make inquiries as to how they got to be in such a blessed state. The Jews would then lead them to a knowledge of the living God! But, you know their history. Because of turning away from God time after time and adopting many of the predominant pagan practices of the people around them, the Hebrew people were carried away captive from their home to a land over 1,000 miles away. It was, ironically, the Babylonian Kingdom that God used to teach them an eternal lesson.

Around 607 years before the birth of Christ in that stable a number of choice college-age Hebrew men were captured and carried into Babylon for a special project of the king. Of that number only four remained faithful to God in the foreign land. You are familiar with their names, Shadrach, Meshach, Abednego, and Daniel. Because of their faithfulness and fidelity, God richly blessed them, and made them stand head and shoulders above their classmates. After a three and a half year crash course in language and government, the four faithful Hebrews were given places of responsibility in the Babylonian government. Though captives they were afforded many luxuries and privileges. They were held in high esteem by the young king Nebuchadnezzar. He even allowed them to become apprentice wise men, trainees for cabinet positions.

One night King Nebuchadnezzar awoke with a start! He had just experienced a very disturbing dream. Wide awake, he tried to piece things together. He immediately rang for a servant, and ordered his cabinet leaders into session. These were the top philosophers, psychiatrists, psychologists, astronomers, and astrologists of his day. They were simply referred to as ''the wise men.''

The king told them the problem. He just must have an answer, an interpretation to the dream. The men were flattered. The king asked them for an interpretation of his dream. They had been reminding others of the fact that they could interpret dreams, but, wow, the king wanted an interpretation! So, they asked him to give them the dream and they would give him the correct interpretation.

The young king had not called too many cabinet sessions together since recently taking over the realm from his father Nabopolassar. But history reveals that Nebuchadnezzar was one of the smartest kings ever to rule a kingdom. He told his cabinet leaders that they were all well paid. He repeated their publicized claims. So, he told them that when they gave him the exact dream he would know that they were giving him the correct interpretation.

They really got disturbed. They told the king that this was not a correct way to go about it. They insisted on knowing the dream first. They reminded him that he was young and inexperienced in these matters. They even told him that his father had never made such a demand on any of them ever. But the king saw through their deceptive devices. He gave them an ultimatum. They were to either give him the dream and the interpretation within a certain few hours or they would face death!

Since Daniel, Shadrach, Meshach, and Abednego were all apprentice wise men, this death decree affected them, too. Daniel immediately went right in before the still-awake king. He asked the king for a little time, promising that he would give the king the dream and the interpretation. The sincerity of this outstanding Hebrew touched the king. He granted Daniel the time.

Daniel went back to his cottage, and along with his three friends, he started a prayer meeting. God honored their request. Daniel went back in before the king. As you read of Daniel relating the dream and the meaning, you will embark on one of the most thrilling revelations of "acts in the future," as well as obtaining a knowledge of present critical events taking place right before your very own eyes.

The story is related in the second chapter of Daniel, beginning with the twenty-seventh verse: "Daniel answered in the presence of the king, and said, The secret which the king demanded cannot the wise men, the astrologers, the magicians, the soothsayers, shew unto the king. But there is a God in heaven that revealeth secrets, and maketh known to the King Nebuchadnezzar what shall be in the latter days." In verse 31, Daniel says, "Thou O king, sawest and behold a great image. This image, whose brightness was excellent, stood before thee; and the form thereof was terrible." Verse 32, "This image's head was of fine gold; his breast and arms of silver, his belly and his thighs of brass. His legs of iron, his feet part of iron and part of clay." Verse 34, "Thou sawest till that a stone was cut out without hands, which smote the image upon his feet that were of iron and clay, and brake them to pieces. Then was the iron, the clay, the brass, the silver, and the gold, broken to pieces together, and became like the chaff of the summer threshing floors; and the wind carried them away, that no place was found for them; and the stone that smote the image became a great mountain, and filled the whole earth."

Nebuchadnezzar listened intently as this young Hebrew, about his own age, related to him exactly what he had seen in his dream. The picture Daniel painted of a huge man, head of gold, chest and arms of silver, stomach and thighs of brass, legs of iron and feet of clay and iron combined, was the exact duplicate of the man Nebuchadnezzar had seen. It did not dawn on the king, at first, that the One who had given him the dream was the same One who gave the same picture with an interpretation to Daniel.

Daniel was relating the picture of the statue of the odd-looking man to the king, and the king was feeling more and more like he would soon know what it all meant. A man made of gold, silver, brass, iron, and clay being struck by a stone that was miraculously cut out of a mountain. Then Daniel relates the meaning of it all. "Thou O king, art a king of kings! For the God of heaven hath given thee a kingdom, power and strength and glory. And wheresoever the children of men dwell, the beast of the field hath He given into thine hand, and hath made thee ruler over them all. Thou art this head of gold!"

Nebuchadnezzar was on the edge of his seat. he could hardly contain himself. He was that head of gold! What did it all mean? Daniel says, "And after thee shall arise another kingdom inferior to thee, and another third kingdom of brass, which shall bear rule over all the earth. And the fourth kingdom shall be strong as iron; forasmuch as iron breaketh in pieces and subdueth all things; and as iron that breaketh all these, shall it break in pieces and bruise."

Then verse 45, "Forasmuch as thou sawest that the stone was cut out of the mountain without hands, and that it break in pieces the iron, the brass, the clay, the silver, and the gold; the great God hath made known to the king what shall come to pass hereafter; and the dream is certain, and the interpretation thereof sure."

This is fantastic. The dream given to Nebuchadnezzar of that statue of the man is a prophecy of world-controlling empires.

Nebuchadnezzar is pictured as king of that first world-controlling empire, and you know that it was the Babylonian Empire. Can you recall the second empire that ruled the world? It was a cooperative government, ruled jointly by the Medes and the Persians. It is called the Medo-Persian Empire.

Artists, who portray the statue, picture the man crossing his arms across his chest similar to that of Sitting Bull. The reason for that is that the two powers united together in overthrowing the mighty Babylonian Empire. The Medo-Persian Empire was perfectly represented in this prophecy. The folded arms represent a joint venture.

You will also recall that the Medo-Persian Empire was conquered by the swift and mighty Grecian army under Alexander the Great. The men of Greece did rise to great prominence. The third world-controlling power was definitely the great Grecian Empire. And, of course, the fourth world power was Rome.

Daniel said that each of these empires, weaker than the power before it, would be destroyed. Babylon fell to the Medes and Persians. The Medo-Persian Empire was taken over by the Grecian Empire. And the roaring Roman Empire ruled fourth. Exactly as God had predicted it would over 400 years in advance! But there is more!

If you happen to remember any of your ancient and world history you might recall that the Roman Empire eventually became divided into ten smaller divisions, ten nations, and they were never able to get back together into one world power, ever. They never did get along. You might be amazed to learn that not only did the Bible accurately prophesy the rise and fall of these four empires, it even minutely described the division of the Roman Empire. Daniel told King Nebuchadnezzar, ''And whereas thou sawest the feet and toes, part of potter's clay and part of iron, the kingdom (Rome) shall be divided, but there shall be in it of the strength of the iron, forasmuch as thou sawest the iron mixed with miry clay. And as the toes of the feet were of iron, and part of clay, so the kingdom shall be partly strong and partly broken.''

Just as sure as the four kingdoms came into existence and faded again, exactly as the Bible said it would, when Rome was divided into what is now a prominent section of Europe some of the nations were stronger than the others. The prophecy did not miss!

Speaking of a knowledge of ancient and world history, you might also remember that these kings of Europe did everything they could to weld the empire back together again. They even went so far as to marry their sons and daughters to daughters and sons of other kings. But that did not work. Look at how the prophecy even spelled out that little gem, ''And whereas thou sawest iron mixed with miry clay, they shall mingle themselves with the seed (children) of men; but, they shall not cleave one to another, even as iron is not mixed with clay.''

How about that? That is pretty plain. Even though the language of the book of Daniel over 2,500 years ago is slightly different from ours today, we can still grasp it all.

The next words of Daniel are going to start to get close to home. You will now see how twenty centuries ago Daniel got a glimpse of your day. ''And in the days of these kings (the ten toes, the divided European nations) shall the God of heaven set up a kingdom, which shall never be destroyed; and the kingdom shall not be left to other people, but it shall break in pieces and consume all these kingdoms, and it shall stand forever. Forasmuch as thou sawest that the stone was cut of the mountain without hands, and that it break in pieces the iron, the brass, the

94

clay, the silver and the gold, the great God hath made known to the king what shall come to pass hereafter; and the dream is certain (dependable) and the interpretation there of sure (or true).''

You can see this clearly, this stone that Nebuchadnezzar saw being miraculously cut out of the mountain without human hands accomplishing it is God's assurance to you that after the fall of pagan Rome no other power will ever, again, rule the world! No communistic or capitalist government will control planet earth.

God says that after these four empires have ruled, the next world-wide leadership will be that of Christ Jesus. God, in His Word, states that Jesus Christ will be the One who will usher in an everlasting kingdom. A kingdom different from all others before it. A kingdom of righteousness and peace forever!

There are some earnest ministers who are untiringly carrying on a campaign against communism. A closer look at Bible prophecy might cause a shifting of their valuable time and energy towards other worthwhile causes. You see, according to the unfailing promises of God in this, and other similar prophecies, Russia, Red China, nor any other nation or power will ever rule the world. The next world-controlling empire will belong to Jesus!

That took care of the first dream. Nebuchadnezzar had that one. In the second dream it is Daniel who experiences it. His dream is recorded in chapter seven. Beginning with the very first verse, ''In the first year of Belshazzar, king of Babylon, Daniel had a dream and visions of his head upon his bed.'' This was a number of years after Daniel had interpreted Nebuchadnezzar's dream, and a lot of things have happened to Daniel. He was promoted, as a reward by Nebuchadnezzar, to vice president of Babylon. He did such an outstanding job with God's blessings that each new king kept him in that position. Nebuchadnezzar is dead. Belshazzar is his grandson. Daniel has a lot on his mind, and God adds more, ''Then he wrote the dream, and told the sum of the matters.''

Nebuchadnezzar could not remember his entire dream. Daniel was making sure that he did not forget one small minute detail of his own dream.

"Daniel spake and said, I saw in my vision by night, and, behold, the four winds (north, east, west and south, from which we get the word "news") of the heaven (the atmosphere) strove upon the great sea. And four great beasts came up from the sea, diverse (or different) one from another. The first was like a lion, and had eagle's wings." As Daniel dreamed he saw four odd-looking animals coming up out of the water. Each one was different from the other. The first animal was a lion, but it had two wings of an eagle. Then he adds, "And, behold, another beast, a second, like to a bear . . . it had three ribs in the mouth of it between the teeth of it; and they said thus to it, Arise, devour much flesh."

The second animal coming up out of the sea was a bear that had three ribs of some other animal clutched between its great teeth. These animals are hard to picture. But, instead of getting more simple they get more complex.

"After this I beheld, and lo, another, like a leopard, which had upon the back of it four wings of a fowl. The beast also had four heads; and dominion was given to it."

Can you picture that? A four-headed leopard with four large bird wings! It is not that complicated when you think it through. These are symbols, and symbols in Bible prophecy are another way of using comic-like illustrations to portray a great and vital truth.

I know that by now you have probably figured out that this dream of Daniel's is the same prophecy as the statue. Daniel's dream has more detail. Examine those first three animals.

The first was the lion. I am sure you have heard of the lion being called "the king of beasts." Babylon's king was called by Daniel "the king of kings." All over ancient Babylonian palaces, in Babylonian writings, and even in their common building bricks, were pictures of the lion with eagle's wings. Since the lion is the king of beasts and the eagle the king of fowls, this combination was a perfect picture of the great strength and long range coverage of the Babylonians.

Then, second, there was the bear with three ribs in its mouth. Just like the chest and arms of the male statue that represented the Medo-Persian Empire, the bear picture agrees. In order for the Medo-Persian power to conquer Babylon, it first had to overcome two other powers, Lydia and Egypt. So the three ribs represent Babylon, Lydia, and Egypt being devoured by the two-fold empire.

Third, there was the four-headed, four-winged leopard. It is quite interesting that the leopard had four heads and not two or three. Since this is the same power Nebuchadnezzar was told would rule the world third, it has to be Greece under Alexander the Great. Okay, but what do these four heads represent?

When Alexander the Great had conquered the world in record-breaking time, it was a marvel to the world. I guess his speed in becoming the third world-ruling power was why hundreds of years before God predicted it all by using the leopard, the swift-footed animal. Alexander the Great became depressed because he had nearly nothing left to conquer. Being an alcoholic anyway, he literally drank himself to death. He died two months before he became 33 years old from a drunken debauchery. They put his body in a glass coffin, embalmed his body in honey, and took him back to the town named after him, Alexandria. After some internal problems in the empire, his four generals took over the kingdom, dividing the territory into four nearly equal parts. They kept it alive for a while working jointly.

The four wings on the already-fast leopard portrayed the amazing speed in which Alexander would conquer the then-known world, and the four heads represent the four divisions the empire was divided into.

Bible prophecy is really fantastic! Daniel's dream tells the same thing as King Nebuchadnezzar's, only with more detail. Now the detail becomes vital as Daniel unfolds the fourth animal in his dream. "After this I saw in the night visions, and behold a fourth beast dreadful and terrible, and strong exceedingly; and it had great iron teeth; it devoured and brake in pieces, and stamped the residue (the left overs from being broken and eaten) with the feet of it; and it was diverse (different) from all the beasts that were before it; and it had ten horns." How many toes did Nebuchadnezzar's male statue have? Sure, ten! So it is the same empire Daniel told the king the legs, feet, and toes represented. It is pagan Rome. Once in a while some writer will come along and declare that the fourth animal in Daniel's dream represents something, or someone, else. Just so you would not be mistaken the Lord sends an angel to Daniel's side and gives him the explanation of the dream. In Daniel 7:23 the angel tells him, "The fourth beast shall be the fourth kingdom upon earth." So, it cannot be any country, organization or power other than the one history absolutely confirms ruled the world fourth, the Roman Empire.

About 100 years before Daniel was given this important dream the Lord spoke to humanity through Amos and said, "Surely the Lord God will do nothing, but he revealeth His secret unto His servants the prophets." Amos 3:7.

The Lord did not leave you alone to fall for Satan's counterfeit. He has given you several outstanding prophecies of all this arch-enemy will do before the end of time. As Daniel is being vividly told of future events you will see how Lucifer is planning to bring about the world-wide hoax that will eventually swindle countless millions of human beings. The Lord even spells out to you, hundreds of years before it hits full speed, this amazing hoax. Read it now, and brace yourself for some stunning revelations.

Daniel was given the answer to the dream of the king's. He is told about the first four beasts in his own dream and it makes sense. But the events that occur after the fall of the fourth empire really send Daniel into a tailspin. He just cannot fathom it all. So, the angel comes to him and starts to piece it all together.

Daniel is looking at the ten horns of the fourth beast. This, of course, is the division that was to take place at Rome's downfall. He says, "I considered the horns (I stared at them and tried to figure them out.) and behold, there came up among them another little horn before whom there were three of the first horns plucked up by the roots; and behold, in this horn were eyes like the eyes of man, and a mouth speaking great things."

As he looked intently at the ten horns of that last animal all of a sudden, one small horn starts to sprout up! As it is growing right before Daniel's eyes, it plucks up three horns. The little horn knocks three of the ten horns up by their roots. What could it possibly be? Now remember, Daniel had already pictured to the king the division of the Roman Empire into ten smaller nations. He understood what the ten horns meant—a division of the empire into ten sections. So, he was looking at the ten horns, and even though he did not know them by name, he was actually seeing the division of Rome into what we know now as Western Europe.

What would a little horn represent that would come into Western Europe and destroy three of its nations in the process?

The horn had human eyes and a mouth. It was saying terrible (or blasphemous) things.

And if Daniel was not already puzzled by this horn with a human mouth and eyes wiping out three other horns, imagine his bewilderment as the little horn did more amazing things.

In verses 21 and 22, Daniel says, "I beheld and the same horn made war with the saints and prevailed against them; until the Ancient of Days came, and judgment was given to the saints of the Most High, and the time came that the saints possessed the kingdom."

Daniel was over his head! He did not know what was going on. The angel gives him some facts that he accepted but did not really understand. All of this was to happen "in the last days," and that means in your time. As you

99

look at these facts you will be able to see how they did come to pass exactly as the Bible said it would. What is more, you will also see how this "little horn" is at work this very moment. And what is even more, you will be able to fully understand how Satan plans to bring off this tremendous hoax. Only you will be able to see it easier than Daniel did!

The angel speaks to Daniel and says, "And another shall arise after them (the little horn coming up after the ten are established), and he shall be diverse . . . and he shall subdue three kings (or kingdoms or nations). And he shall speak great words against the Most High (God Almighty) and shall wear out the saints of the Most High (the true Christians); and think to change times and laws. And they (the Christians) shall be given into his hand until a time, times, and the dividing of times; but the judgment will sit (justice will win out), and they (the Christians) will take away his dominion, to consume and destroy it to the end. And the kingdom and the dominion and the greatness of the kingdom under the whole heaven will be given to the people of the saints of the Most high, whose kingdom is an everlasting kingdom; and all dominions shall serve and obey Him (the Lord)".

Maybe, right now you are as confused as I was when I first tried to make sense out of it all. As you look it over it will all come clear. Look at the prophecy.

First, after pagan Rome falls there will come along another power represented by that little horn.

Second, that little horn power is to grow to become a world-influencing force, different from all the empires before it.

Third, it is to proclaim defying words against God.

Fourth, it would "think" or propose to change God's eternal laws.

Fifth, it would cause Christians to be persecuted, to experience pain, perplexity and imprisonment.

Sixth, its influence over the world would continue for a

100

certain, specified time, be set back, and then, once again, grow world-wide.

Seventh, the little horn power will eventually be destroyed forever.

The tragedy in all this is the overwhelming number the Bible reveals will be swept under the deceptive and destructive influence of this little horn system before the end! Many New Testament prophecies are explicit in describing the little horn power and the gigantic mass of humans that lose eternal life through its magnetic power.

In Revelation 13:8 that gigantic number of deceived humans is defined this way, ''And all that dwell upon the earth shall worship him (the little horn power), whose names are not written in the book of life of the Lamb slain from the foundation of the world.''

When you think of the fact that the majority of humans will be lost as a result of this terrible power, it becomes critical for you to discover who this is! It is vital that you discover the truth regardless of how many concepts you might have to change! When you consider the fact that much of the book of Revelation deals with this prophecy, spelling it out to you, warning you that even you could be misled and lose out on eternal life, you must search for the Biblical answer as to who this power really is. You have to protect yourself from its damning and deadly deceptions. You cannot afford to become another of its millions of victims!

One day, the Bible says, it will be controlling practically all lives on earth. All lives, that is, except those who prepare, study, and pray this thing through to its Biblical conclusion. It could control your life. Think of that! Not one single person will be exempt. It will be either a right relationship with Christ and his teachings, or a duped and deceived follower of this anti-Christian system. The result will be either eternal life or eternal damnation. You will be either one who is victorious over it through Christ, or one who is without Christ right in the middle of it all.

So what you have to determine is this: Who is this

power? How can you keep from being eternally lost through its teachings and power? As you will see later, this power will one day soon place the entire world where each person must make a decision where the outcome will determine that person's life or death. You must determine correctly and unbiasedly exactly who the Bible predicts will do it all.

You have heard that old saying that "you can fool some of the people some of the time, but you can't fool all of the people all of the time." That same psychology is the very method in figuring out who this little horn power is. Some powers and people can fit some of the clues some of the time. But you have to nail down the one power that fits all these descriptive clues all the time. Look carefully at the clues you were given.

First, this power was to rise after the fall of pagan Rome, when a division into ten smaller nations took place.

The Roman Empire fell as a result of internal turmoil as well as many barbarian countries waging war against it. A long seige by these barbarians divided the empire into ten segments, ten parts. Some of the barbarian countries took bigger "pieces of the pie", so to speak, than others, but the result was an empire split into ten sections. Even though the names may not mean much to you now, they were as follows:

Ostrogoths, Visigoths, Franks, Suevi, Alamanni Vandals, Anglo-saxons, Heruli, Lombards, and Burgundians.

These were the ten toes in Nebuchadnezzar's male statue, and also the ten horns in Daniel's beast. You will grasp the full significance of these ten countries as you take a brief refresher course in world history.

In the early days of the Christian Church the born-again believers sacrificed everything they had in the way of time, talent, and treasure to see the gospel story go to the whole world. Each local church selected its own officers and leaders. The individual church took care of its own church buildings, conducted its own missionary endeavors, and ran their own church schools. They were autonomous, self-governed, and self-supporting.

The leader of a local church was placed in that position solely on the basis of his Christ-like character and zeal for winning souls.

When these churches started to experience the "falling away" as the Apostle Paul predicted would happen, they started adopting more and more of the prevailing sun-worshipping practices. As these pagan concepts were slowly being woven into their rules and regulations, the high standard of Christian morality began to lower, the dynamic preaching about the risen Lord was watered down, and more and more ceremony, display, and formalism put simplicity out the door!

With so many sun worshippers infiltrating the church, it was not too long before wealthy and prominent pagan men were actually leading the churches!

On several occasions a few churches pooled its powers together for certain projects with success. Soon other groups of churches were doing the same thing. Many social benefits derived from these cooperating churches. This led to the eventual formation of groups of churches all across the land.

These groups of churches also had leaders. The leader of a group of churches was called a "bishop." The church was "organized" now with little conferences and branches all across the land, and each group with its own "bishop" presiding over it.

Since most "bishops" were all basically sun worshippers in spite of their positions with the church, this led to several serious downfalls.

A teaching swept through these conferences of churches that since the "bishops" were full-time students of spiritual things, and devoted much time in prayer, their prayers could get better results than the average working man or his busy family. So, not too long after Jesus had died to make a direct access to God through Him, the church had accepted the doctrine of the priestly ministry, where one man prayed in behalf of many others.

Another serious downfall came about through these "bishops". Since they were worldly men with their deep sun worshipping backgrounds, there soon arose a spirit of competition among them. Each man tried to out shine the other. The more churches he had under his control the more important he was in the circle of bishops. A fierce struggle began. Each man strove to see who could get the largest territory, and derive the largest income. The one bishop who did wind up in the top position was the bishop of Rome. It was the most prominent and prosperous city in the entire then-known world. So Rome became the headquarters of the whole church.

When the Roman Empire was divided into those ten nations with odd names, some of them had adopted the teachings of the church, but some had not.

The church had a big friend in Justinian. Justinian waged war against all nations not accepting the church's teachings. After a series of hard battles and difficult wars it all boiled down to three hold-out nations. One by one those three nations, who prevented the church from being a complete world power, were put down. The last one brought to ruin was in the year 538 A.D.

In 538 A.D. Justinian had broken the last three non-conforming nations. They were the Heruli, the Vandals, and the Ostrogoths.

So, then, this power, that was a combination of a little Christianity and a lot of sun worship, was established. It occurred exactly as the Bible said it would, after the fall of pagan Rome, in 538 A.D.

The second clue is easily understood now. It was to be "different" from all the other world powers. Since Babylon, Medo-Persia, Greece, and Rome had all been military powers, it would have to be a religious or political power. But, stranger than that was the fact that it was both! It was religious and political. It was "different."

Then, the third clue is also understandable. It was to

"speak great words against the Most High." To bring into Christianity all those mystical, mythical, pagan sun-worshipping rules, and lewd rituals was, of course, a damaging assault against God. The New English Bible says this power would "hurl defiance at the Most High." So, the prophecy indicates, among other things, that turning men's hearts and minds away from the Creator to those created objects of worship on earth and in the heavens, that leading humans away from observing the Lord's time schedule, that turning them from keeping that sanctified holy day of rest and worship to the pagan day of the sun, that substituting pagan concepts for the true and simple gospel, and that by using power and arms to force obedience and allegiance in the place of the magnetic attraction of a new-birth experience in Christ, would be one of the clues that the power was the little horn attacking the Creator.

The fourth clue is also very easy to understand. It said that the little horn would "wear out the saints of the Most High."

Now it did not say that it would destroy the saints! It said it would "wear out." In other words it would be a slow, persistent, continual process of breaking down and subduing.

Historians tell us that after 538 A.D. the world experienced a long, long period called "The Dark Ages." This extended time was called "the dark ages" because of the dark spiritual ignorance that was prevalent during that time. No one had the Bible to read. Only the church leaders were permitted to have copies. And those who had them were so deep in sun worship that it had no effect on them. Only in an isolated case here and there, where a few families had secreted themselves in the mountain caves and isolated wildernesses, was the Bible ever truly read and prayed over.

The continual presentation of pagan, mythical, and superstitious teachings wrapped in the cover of Christianity wore away at the spirituality of the people.

There were some people who openly refused to accept

105

these counterfeit teachings and they, of course, were tortured with the hopes that they would change their thinking. The refusal to change brought more torture. If, at the point of death these dissenters still continued to refuse, they were killed. Most of them died under unbelievable pressure and pain. We are told that during the dark ages more than fifty million lost their lives.

Now comes one of the most fantastic prophecies about this little horn power. This persecution and "wearing out the saints of the Most High" was to last until the little horn power was paralyzed and put out of commission for a while. Get this, now, that little horn was to continue in its world-wide influence for "a time, times and the dividing of times." And this is amazing!

After a lot of research I found out that I did not have to research at all outside the Bible for the key to this puzzling time prophecy. The Bible had the solution in it all the time and I did not know it!

You see, "time" in Bible prophecy equals one year. It is not one year of literal time as we know it, but a year in prophetic time. The man who showed me how to figure this out must have thought I was not all there mentally, but when it came clear once again I thought about how stupid I was when it came to a knowledge of the Bible.

Here it is. In the Bible there are no months with 31 days in them. There are no 28 day months either. All Biblical months have the same number of days in them. All Biblical months have 30 days! So, there are 360 days in each year. The Jewish people observing this time period as the Bible truly teaches, still maintain those 360 days. That is why their New Year's Day comes at different times than that of our country's. Some feel the Jewish calendar is more true and dependable than ours. Whether or not it is is not important here. Anyway, "time" would consist of one year or prophetic time, or one year of 360 days of prophecy.

When you add this prophecy of "time, times, and the dividing of time" it sure does make sense. "Time" equals 360. "Times" would be twice that amount, or 720 days.

106

"Dividing of times" would be half a time, or 180. Add these figures of 360, 720, and 180 and you will have a total of 1,260.

If you are a little confused, what you will see next will make you even more until you put it all together.

In Numbers 14:34 and Ezekiel 4:6 you have two examples of how one day in Bible prophecy equals a literal year. This is in Bible prophecy only, and not every time the Bible speaks of simply a year.

So, in this prophecy of the little horn continuing in power and influence for a "time, times, and the dividing of time," you actually have a prophecy of a total time of 1,260 prophetic days. Since a day in Bible prophecy equals a year, this power was to continue until its temporary paralysis, for 1,260 actual years.

Just to make sure that this is all correct and not an assumption, the Bible confirms this time period in several places. In Revelation 12:14 it speaks of the true church during that dark ages period having to flee away from it all for "a time, times, and half a time." But, in the sixth verse of the same chapter it spells it out as: "A thousand, two hundred and threescore days." A "score" is 20, so "threescore would be 60. That totals, again, 1,260! To make sure there is no mistake, the thirteenth chapter of Revelation speaks of this little horn system and it says, "And power was given unto him to continue forty and two months." Forty-two months with 30 days in each month also equals 1,260 prophetic days!

Now, back to the prophecy so you will see it as clear as crystal. It predicts that this little horn system would be allowed to do all these things for 1,260 years. Since it has been established that the fallen church system came into full power in 538 A.D., if you add 1,260 years to that you will have a total of 1798. Okay, looking to history you will find an astonishing event taking place in 1798. Do you know what it was? I must have skipped school the day this was discussed because I did not realize it until I saw it several places in the most reliable historical writings and

107

even in some better encyclopedias. Do you have any idea what it was? Before you look at this stunning solution, you need to remember two very vital things.

First, when you have been raised to believe a certain way, or to believe in certain things, and you are honest and sincere, you accept those beliefs and practices without any questions. You love your parents and your parents' parents. You respect them, and you respect their beliefs. And as a result of this, the largest majority of people follow in their parents' footsteps as far as religion is concerned. You are probably in this class of sincere people. Most of us are. So, until you come face to face with a test of your beliefs, you never, ever, think that these beliefs could ever be anything but one hundred percent Biblical. So unless you see something within the framework of your belief that causes you to wonder, or unless you feel an emptiness from some of the teachings, rituals and services within that framework, you will always stay contented there. In other words, the majority go to the places of worship out of custom, habit, and tradition rather than from the result of a diligent search of the Scriptures. Very few are associated with their religious organizations as a result of real earnest sessions of prayer for guidance coupled with that deep study.

The second vital thing to remember is that the Bible is dealing with organizations, not individuals, in these prophecies. Just as the Jewish nation is no more the chosen people of God, every single individual Jew is still loved deeply by God and can come to a knowledge of, and a right relationship with Christ Jesus. The Bible, in this great prophecy, is not dealing with the true, sincere, Christ-loving men, women, and children within an organization that experienced a certain "falling away" for a time. Now, to that 1798 event!

You have heard of the French Revolution which began in 1789, overthrew the French monarchy, and ended in the Empire of Napoleon I. During the Revolution the French Directory ordered Pope Pius VI to surrender the temporal government. He refused. One of Napoleon's top generals, Berthier, marched victoriously into the city, had the Pope dragged from the altar. His rings were torn from his fingers, and he was carried prisoner into Tuscany. The Pope died in August of 1799, at the age of 82! But the date of Berthier's outrageous actions was February 10, 1798! The pontifical government was paralyzed—February 10, 1798!

Now, before you decide who the little horn power is, look at the other clues in this prophecy.

The little horn was to "think to change times and laws." You have already seen how the basic Bible time schedule has been changed from counting a day from sunset to sunset to the pagan time of from midnight to midnight. That change might not seem to be a terrible sin, but nevertheless it did change it and the change was based strictly upon a foundation of sun worship. And, as you know, sun worship is a direct violation of God's teachings as well as a direct denial of God Himself! You have also learned that the Lord created a special day for man. That day was sanctified, made holy, and set apart for one purpose and one purpose only. It was to be a halting of secular work and activities, and a time for physical rest, spiritual refreshment, and reviving. The observance of that day is a definite command of God in His law. It, too, like the reckoning of time, was altered on a sun-worshipping foundation.

And the change of that day to the sun-day has now become an almost total acceptance by Christianity. And it has all been through the consent and approval of two gigantic organizations. Look at what those two organizations have to say in their defense.

I guess that you know that the first organization is the Roman Catholic Church.

And the second organization consenting and approving of the change of the Sabbath from the seventh to the first day of the week is, with a few isolated exceptions, the great body of the Protestant Churches. The first group, the

Catholic Church readily admits that they made that change. One illustration, typical of all such written proclamations, makes this very clear. Peter Gierman, wrote a book entitled "Convert's Catechism of Catholic Doctrine," and on page 50, he states this, "We observe Sunday instead of Saturday because the Catholic Church in the Council of Laodicea transferred the solemnity from Saturday to Sunday."[8]

In Holtzman's book, "Canon and Tradition," he spells it out very clearly, "The Church has changed the Sabbath into Sunday, not by the command of Christ, but by its own authority."[9]

This was not a surprise at all to me because of the knowledge of these things my research had given me. You have already gained that same knowledge from what you have read in this book thus far. But, you will never, ever, be able to find the adjectives and superlatives to describe my absolute bewilderment when I read a statement of a Protestant author, and minister, made to four thousand fellow ministers in a large meeting in New York City on November 13, 1893. The man was Dr. Edward T. Hiscox, the author of the Baptist Manual. Listen to this stunning declaration: "Of course, I quite well know that Sunday did come into use in the early Christian history as a religious day as we have learned from the Christian fathers and others. But, what a pity that it comes branded with the mark of paganism and christened with the name of the sun god, when adopted and sanctioned by the papal apostasy, and bequeathed as a sacred legacy to Protestantism."

Can you imagine a leading Baptist theologian actually making that confession? After I got over the mental shock, I wondered how in the world 4,000 ministers listened to his words, heard the facts, and then did nothing whatsoever about it?

You read a few confessions from Protestant ministers in an earlier chapter, but one more will really add to the complete bewilderment! Let me tell you where this next statement is taken from before you read it. It is from the book, "The Ten Commandments," by Cannon Eaton,

Church of England. Man, to read this from a good Episcopalian preacher is still a stunning experience. Here it is: "There is no work, no hint in the New Testament about abstaining from work on Sunday. The observance of Ash Wednesday and Lent, stand exactly on the same footing as the observance of Sunday."

Even the Lutheran Church, the one Protestants point to as their father church, makes such an equally amazing confession, "The observance of the Lord's day Sunday, is founded not on any Commandment of God, but on the authority of the Church." Augsburg confession of faith quoted in Catholic Sabbath Manual, part 2, chapter 1, Section 10.

I could give you a list as long as my arm of statements similar to these you have just read. But, the point I am trying to make must be very clear. Protestants and Catholics, alike, readily admit that the change of God's law, as prophesied it would take place, has taken place!

The Bible predicts a great deal about these two organizations and the role each play in this great eternal act on earth's stage. You are in for some very unusual reading in further chapters.

But, back to the prophecy before us. At this particular juncture, the prophecy is pointing primarily to that one organization initially responsible for an attempted change in God's law. It said, "think to change times and laws." And you have seen how that thinking has been carried out, with a few exceptions, with very good success!

The Bible says that the little horn power would attempt to change times and laws, and your history books are full of substantiating proof of how this change did take place. The changing of the seventh-day Sabbath into the day of the sun was just one of the violations of God's law that took place.

When Moses stood trembling before the thunder and lightning and smoke of Mount Sinai, the Lord struck stone with His finger and engraved ten regulations, ten codes, ten rules for success for man, for all times. You know

111

them as the Ten Commandments. You might be shocked a little more as you compare the original ten given by the Lord, as found in Exodus 20:3–17 and the ten listed in the Catholic Catechism.

The first commandment goes like this, "Thou shalt have no other gods before me." In the first commandment listed in the catechism are these words, "Thou shalt have no strange gods before me." Well, that is very little different and nothing is lost, is there? But, look at the second commandment God gave and then the catechism's version. It goes like this, "Thou shalt not make unto thee any graven image, or any likeness of anything that is in heaven above, or that is in the earth beneath, or that is in the water under the earth; thou shalt not bow down thyself to them, nor serve them. . . ." Here is the other version, "Thou shalt not take the name of God in vain." What happened? The one just quoted as the second commandment is actually the third one God gave mankind. It is completely left out! Why? You see, when the church was invaded by the gigantic number of sun worshippers it was soon overwhelmed with problems. The massive number of sun worshippers had had their visible objects, their statues and idols, in their religious services. They wanted them again in the church! And, with the majority being sun worshippers it is easy to see how these were incorporated as a part of Christian worship and ritual. Many of the pagan idols were simply renamed to give them a Christian air! Nevertheless, during the dark ages, the church did alter the original plan of the Lord to include the pagan concepts of visible objects of worship.

Now, when you take one commandment away from ten you will be left with just nine. The church could not publicize just nine! So, each of the commandments was pushed up. That is, the third commandment became the second, the fourth became the third, the fifth the fourth, the sixth the fifth, the seventh the sixth, the eighth the seventh, the ninth the eighth. And in one of the most ingenious swift strokes of pen and ink, the tenth commandment was divided into two parts. It originally read this way, "Thou shalt not covet thy neighbor's house, thou shalt not covet thy neighbor's wife, nor his manservant, nor his maidservant, nor his ox, nor his ass, nor anything that is thy neighbor's." The tenth commandment was a strict censure against the sin of lust. The sun-worshipping leaders at that council session simply made the first part of the tenth commandment to become the ninth one in their books. It read "Thou shalt not covet thy neighbor's house." Then the remainder of the tenth commandment, or part of it, was used to make up their tenth one. It simply reads, "Thou shalt not covet thy neighbor's wife."

When the second commandment cut diametrically across their newly founded practice of idols, the council actually connived together to not change their practices, but to change the law of God!

By the way, it was this same altered ten commandments that Martin Luther taught after he had broken away from the church! He was never made aware of that original change.

So, then, as difficult as it is to state, and maybe as it is even more difficult to accept, the Bible has pinpointed the little horn! It was to "rise up after the fall of pagan Rome." And the little horn power did come into full power in the year 538 A.D. when those three non-conforming nations were destroyed.

It was to persecute Christians and it really did! Everyone is familiar with the little horn's persecutions. But, get this now, those persecutions lasted from 538 to 1798. And from 538 to 1798 is exactly 1,260 years! You remember that the prophecy said it was to make war against the saints of the Most High for that "time, times, and dividing of time." That calculation equalled exactly 1,260 years. And that fits historical facts to a "T!"

The little horn power was to "be different" from all other powers before it. The four world-controlling powers were all military. But the Roman Church was both religious and political!

113

It was to be guilty of blasphemy. One of the cardinal doctrines of Christianity has been through the years the great substitutionary death of Jesus for you and me. Jesus died that you and I might not face eternal death! In the book of Hebrews this theme is repeated over and over again. One element in that repetition needs to be looked at closely. In Hebrews 9:28 notice the words, "So Christ was once offered to bear the sins of many."

In Hebrews 10:10, notice the repetition and see if you can spot the important element, "By the which will we are sanctified through the offering of the body of Jesus Christ once for all."

In Hebrews 10:12, notice one more of the many repetitions and that same vital element, "But this Man (Jesus) after He had offered one sacrifice for sins forever, sat down on the right hand of God." You found that crucial element, did you not? It was the doctrine that Christ's death on the cross was "once for all," "was once offered," and "offered one sacrifice." One time was all that was needed for Divinity to substitute for man. Jesus had to die only one perfect death. It has been finished! Nothing else on Christ's part is needed. A recently published book, "Faith of Millions," deals with the Roman doctrine of the mass. It speaks of the priests power and this is what it says, "Indeed it (the power of the priest) is greater than the power of the Virgin Mary. While the blessed virgin was the human agency by which Christ became incarnate a single time, the priest brings Christ down from heaven, and renders Him present on our altar as the eternal victim for the sins of man—not once, but, a thousand times!" It continues, "The priest speaks and lo! Christ, the eternal, omnipotent God, bows His head in humble obedience to the priest's command."[10] You see, the Creator is made a slave to His creatures! The teaching, then, completely ignores the Biblical fact of one single death. It makes the priest more powerful than the Lord Jesus Christ!

You have already learned that "blasphemy" is two

things: first, a human claiming to be God, and second, a human claiming power to forgive sins.

In Christopher Marcellus' famous speech at the Fourth Session of the Fifth Lateral Council, he looked directly at the Pontiff and said, "Thou art the Shepherd, thou art the Physician, thou art the Director, thou art the Husbandman, finally thou art another God on earth," and the entire papal government agreed with him.

This is the official claim of the Roman Catholic Church for the Pope: "The Pope alone is deservedly called by the name "Most Holy" because he is the Vicar of Christ, who is the fountain and source and fullness of all holiness. . . . If it were possible that the angels might err in the faith, they could be judged by the Pope. . . . For he is of so great dignity and power that he forms one and the same tribunal with Christ. . . . The Pope is of so great authority and power that he can modify, explain and interpret even divine laws . . ." (Prompta Bibliotheca, Article 2, "Papa.")

Pope Leo XIII's Encyclical Letter "The Reunion of Christendom" said this, "We (the pope) hold upon this earth the place of God Almighty." The Catechism of the Council of Trent For Parish Priests, page 318, is this declaration, "Bishops and priests being, as they are, God's interpreters and ambassadors, empowered in His name to teach mankind the divine law and rules of conduct, and holding, as they do, His place on earth, it is evident that no nobler function than theirs can be imagined. Justly, therefore, are they called not only Angels, but even gods, because of the fact that they exercise in our midst the power and prerogatives of the immortal God."

"In all ages, priests have been held in the highest honor; yet the priests of the New Testament far exceed all others. For the power of consecrating and offering the body of our Lord and of forgiving sins, which has been conferred on them, not only has nothing equal to it on earth, but even surpasses human reason and understanding."[11]

When I read these statements, coupled with the other

fulfilled prophecies about the little horn, my stomach was in knots! Even to this date, as I relate this to someone else, I still feel such a tension that it is impossible to describe. Maybe you have felt a little of that and know what I mean.

The great God of the universe knew full well what was going to take place on earth through the years. He has spelled it all out to you in His prophetic writings in His Book!

He has given you an insight to the fact that Satan will make his supernatural, and I mean "super"-supernatural, efforts to twist the image of the Lord from man's mind. He was going to make his all-out push to cause man to misunderstand the love of God, to misinterpret His message of concern for him, and to misconstrue the mission of salvation by a counterfeit religious force becoming a world-wide influence and power. And by that power lead the world astray. It is of eternal importance that you know these facts and protect yourself from its deadly deceptions.

With only a few exceptions here and there, Christianity has almost lost all of its force and attractiveness through its satanically inspired acceptance of sun-worshipping theories and practices into its own doctrine and rituals.

It is no more that powerful force that turned the world upside down in its early days. With a few exceptions, it is now no more than a cute story for little children and a comfort for the aged and senile! And we Christians have to take the responsibility for this wholesale decline! It is our responsibility.

In the next to the last book of the Bible, the little one chapter book of Jude, Jude wrote to the Christians of his day and said, "Beloved, when I gave all diligence to write unto you of the common salvation, it was needful (or urgent) for me to write unto you, and exhort (or urge) you that ye should earnestly contend (or fight) for the faith that was once delivered unto the saints."

If it was needful then for him to urge his people to return to the true gospel and repel all those sun-worshipping doctrines that were coming into the church, how much more urgent is it for you and me 1900 years later?

The story is told of a midwestern country store that was now under the management of the third generation of men. The owner and manager's father, and his father's father, had all operated the general store. It seems that one day a lady, a regular customer, came in to buy some material and a dress pattern. After selecting the pattern she picked out the material. Taking it to the manager she requested 3 yards. As he had done hundreds of times before, he took the material to the counter and grasping the end of the cloth, he stretched it across the counter from one very familiar thumbtack to the other thumbtack. He repeated the process twice so as to make three yards. You see, the two thumbtacks were traditional items, marking off one yard! Since the cost of material was going up almost every day, he did not, as he usually had done through the years, give an additional two or three inches of extra material. He cut it exactly to the very inch. After all, he had to think about staying in business. And you cannot stay in business unless you make a profit.

The lady took the material home and put the pattern pieces on it. Something was wrong! She tried to readjust the position of the pattern on the material but with no success. Finally she decided that she did not get the full yards.

She returned the material, telling the manager that there must have been a mistake. She did not have enough material. They checked another pattern to see if there had been a mistake in the directions. But, it did call for three yards. So he returned to the counter and spread out the material. He stretched the material from one thumbtack to the other. One yard! He stretched it again. Two yards! Then one last time and, three yards!

"I just don't understand," he said, "You've got three yards, all right."

The lady hesitated and then said, "You measured the

yardage with those two old thumbtacks in the counter. How do you know they're right?"

"Well," the owner replied kindly, "We have used those two tacks ever since this store was first built. My daddy did it. My grandpa did it. And I have done it hundreds of times."

"Well, still," she insisted, "how do you know they're exactly right?"

He said, "Look, I'll measure it for you and prove it."

He walked over to the hardware section and picked up a carpenter's folding rule. He went back over to the counter and confidently placed the end of the ruler at the first tack and stretched it out to the other one. He was shocked beyond words when he saw that the measurement was 34 inches instead of 36! He just could not believe it! He had sold hundreds and hundreds of yards of material with those old measuring tacks! Something was wrong. He rechecked the measurement with a steel measuring tape. But, to his dismay, it, too, revealed 34 inches! Then, it dawned on him. That morning he had decided not to give any extra material because of the cost increase. That had done it. The tacks were wrong. But giving people a few extra inches each time made it almost correct.

Now he was faced with a decision. What would he do? Someone had made a mistake! Would he continue to sell under deceptive practices or would he place them in the correct positions?

What would you do? Of course you would make them correct!

He did that. He went over and tried to pull up one of the tacks. He broke off the end of his fingernail. It was hard to pull up. It had been there for so long it was difficult to change. So, he went over and got a screwdriver and tried to pry it up. But, the head popped off, leaving just the stem. He got a pair of pliers and firmly squeezing them tight around the stem he was able to remove the tack. You see, things that have been deeply imbedded are difficult to change!

When he got a new thumbtack and went to the correct 36-inch mark on the counter, he found another little surprise. When he pushed the tack into the wood, he found that it went in like he had been pressing it into butter. So, he took out his pocketknife and scrapped the old tarnished varnish away from the area. And, there, in the exact 36-inch spot was a very small cork. Someone had deliberately taken the tack out and changed it!

Now, God's Word has warned you that a counterfeit religion was to come into the world. This system would be a combination of sun worship and Christianity. It would incorporate many non-Biblical teachings into its doctrines. It would influence practically all the rest of Christendom to adopt the same mixture. That mixture would cause some radical doctrinal changes. One of the most radical changes has been that of God's holy Sabbath day. But, many more would follow. And now you are faced with a decision. What will you do about these changes? Will you accept them because practically everyone else has, and does or will you be able to "pull up the traditional tacks"?

Martin Luther had a question about a Christian and secular government. He wondered to what extent should secular authority be obeyed. Then the answer came. He said publicly, "But when a prince is in the wrong, are his people bound to follow him then too? I answer, no, for it is not one's duty to do wrong."

In Matthew 15:9 Jesus said something that is very thought-provoking. He said, "But in vain they do worship me, teaching for doctrines the commandments of men."

What other traditional doctrines might very well be the "commandments of men"?

What other changes have been passed on through ancient Babylon to Medo-Persia, and on to Greece and Rome, through Papal Rome and into modern Protestantism, and unknown to you?

What will be the result of these past changes in your future?

What events will take place in the future, not according to God's original plan for mankind, now that these changes have been established and adopted by the biggest majority of earth's population? Does the Bible also predict that?

8/THE INFINITE IMPRINT

Have you ever heard the old saying that, "Good laws lead to the making of better ones, but bad laws only bring about worse ones"? You might have had some stunning shocks in reading the accounts of the world-wide hoax Satan is perpretating on unsuspecting human beings that are "All in the Name of the Lord." But, in the prophecy you are about to encounter, those previous shocks, in comparison, will not even give your mental and spiritual senses a twinge. All that you have read thus far will seem like a Sunday School picnic as you discover one of the most ingenious schemes the arch enemy of your life will ever conceive.

This prophecy, next in the sequence of events to occur before the second coming of Christ, will disclose to you a plot more exciting and thought provoking than any scheme any science fiction author could imagine. The tragedy is that it will not be fiction but an accurate and dependable fact!

You see, this satanic swindle deals with a bad law. This bad law will not only be passed, but it will bring about poverty, privation, and prison for some precious people and the loss of eternal life for the others.

This bad law prophecy is so incredible that there is no human being who can conceive of the adjectives and superlatives to adequately describe its importance and urgency. There is no way to overstress the necessity of

121

studying its minute details because you will be directly and actively engaged in the workings of it. You will be involved in it, whether or not you want to. There is no way to avoid it. Every single person on planet earth's surface will take part in it, in one way or another.

This crucial prophecy is found in the thirteenth chapter of Revelation. It starts off in verse 1 like this: ''And I (John) stood upon the sand of the sea, and saw a beast rise up out of the sea, having seven heads and ten horns, and upon the horns ten crowns, and upon his heads the name of blasphemy.''

You have already gotten a head start in understanding this seemingly strange statement. You have already learned that a ''beast'' in Bible prophecy is simply an animal that represents a military, political or religious power.

Actually, this is not difficult to grasp. We have used these same types of animal symbols for years. For example, who does the lion represent? Sure, it is England. The big bear represents Russia. What animal do we use to represent the United States? We use the eagle and sometimes the buffalo. We even use these animal symbols in political circles. The elephant is the Republican Party, and the Democrats have chosen the donkey.

Now, with this background, look carefully at this symbolic beast. The Bible goes on to describe him more, ''And the beast which I saw was like unto a leopard, and his feet were as the feet of a bear, and his mouth as the mouth of a lion; and the dragon gave him his power and his seat, and great authority.''

From the things you discovered in the prophetic dream of Daniel, this is not as difficult to piece together as it first seems. You recall that the lion portrayed the Babylonian Empire, the bear the Medo-Persian Empire, the leopard the Grecian Empire, and the pagan Roman Empire was portrayed by a very odd beast with ten horns. So, then, this odd beast is a combination of the four powers. In other words, this beast is an outgrowth of those powers and comes along after them. It would possess some of each of their characteristics.

In addition, this new beast has seven heads! On each head is written the word "blasphemy." This will also become clear as you will remember that the leopard that represented the great Grecian Empire under Alexander the Great had four heads. The four heads represented the four generals who took over the empire after Alexander's death. So, a head on a beast in Bible prophecy would represent some type of general, leader, dictator, president, or ruler.

The beast has seven heads. This can mean one of two things. First, there will be seven actual leaders or organizations giving real life and support to the beast power. Second, since the number seven also represents completeness, fullness or perfection, this seven-headed beast may be a picture of some power that all organizations or leaders support completely. You will decide for yourself as you read more. An additional clue as to what type of power this beast represents is in the statement "and upon his heads the name of blasphemy."

Since blasphemy only occurs in the realm of the spiritual, these seven heads have to represent some types of religious powers or organizations.

So, from what has been given you so far is a picture of some religious power that comes along after the fall of the last world-wide empire. This religious power has some of the characteristics of all those empires in it. It is a power that will be supported by either seven distinct religious forces or all the religious powers.

Then, the description of that beast power is enlarged by these words: "And the dragon gave him his power and his seat and great authority." Now the dragon comes into the picture once again. Since you have already learned that the dragon is Satan, you can also figure it all out easily. The Devil inspires this power. He also aids and abets its success. So then, you have a picture of some powerful organization that is not only satanically inspired, but is operating, or will operate, with full support of all the world's religious

123

powers. Since the Bible takes the space to write about it in prophecy, it stands to reason that it will take a real important role in the last day events.

The prophecy now focuses in on one particular religious power who not only takes the leading role in this beast's activities, but goes on to actually take over the whole operation. It states it like this: "And I saw one of his heads as it were wounded to death; and his deadly wound was healed; and all the world wondered after the beast." You also have an idea as to who this wounded head is from the previous study of Daniel's odd beast. To make sure that you do not misinterpret this identification, the prophecy goes into more detail about the one distinct head. It says: "And there was given unto him a mouth speaking great things and blasphemies; and power was given unto him to continue forty and two months."

That power, once again, is the papal heirachy. It did receive a "deadly wound" in 1798, as you have seen. It also regained its power and prestige in 1929 when Mussolini signed a pact with it, restoring all its authority.

Get this, the San Francisco Chronicle published an account of the pact-signing on the front page of its newspaper. It actually read like this, "Mussolini and Gaspari Sign Historic Pact . . . Heal Wound of Many years." That is fantastic! The Bible prophesied that its wound would be healed and the newspaper confirmed it in the exact same words.

The strong head that regained its power and influence cannot be misunderstood or misinterpreted. To make absolutely sure no one who is conscienciously concerned makes a mistake about this identification, the prophecy adds, "And he opened his mouth in blasphemy against God, to blaspheme His name, and His tabernacle, and them that dwell in heaven. And it was given unto him to make war with the saints, and to overcome them."

The key to understanding this puzzle lies in the prophecy itself. You were just told that this power was to blaspheme God. The Bible does not leave anyone who sincerely seeks for an answer without help. Blasphemy is defined within the Bible itself. Blasphemy is made up of two things. Both of these two are found in two incidents in the life of Christ.

The first one is found in the second chapter of Mark. You are probably familiar with the story. Jesus had gone into a certain home in Capernaum. When the townfolk heard that He was there, they began to crowd into the home bringing all their sick and dying loved ones. Jesus began to heal these pitiful people.

Four men came to the home carrying a very ill man on his mattress. When they got there they saw that it was impossible to get inside. So, they went up on the roof, took off a large number of roof tiles, and made a hole through which they could lower this man, bed and all, into the home. After a great deal of difficulty, they were able to carefully lift the man up onto the top of the house. Taking ropes and tying them to the four corners of the thin mattress, they were able to lower him slowly down into the very room where Jesus was performing His wonderful healing acts.

Jesus was overwhelmed by the compassion of these four men for their sick friend. The King James Version says he had palsy. But in its original Greek it was paralysis. This has to be correct because a man with palsy could have, with assistance, walked into the house. Nevertheless, when Jesus thought about the man's faith and the trouble he went through, He was deeply impressed.

The Bible says that Jesus turned to the man on the mattress and said, "Son, thy sins be forgiven thee."

The religious leaders were shocked. In verse seven they said to each other, "Why doth this man thus speak blasphemies? Who can forgive sins but God only?"

Jesus questioned them and asked if it was easier to simply say that a person's sins were forgiven or to heal that person. Then Jesus said, "But that ye may know that the Son of man hath power on earth to forgive sins, He saith to the sick of the palsy, Arise, and take up thy bed, and go thy way into thine house." And the man did it! So, the first thing that makes up blasphemy is for a human being to claim that he can forgive sins.

The second thing making up blasphemy is found in the twenty-sixth chapter of Matthew. The high priest had demanded that Jesus confess if He was the Son of God or not. Then Jesus said that He was. In verse 65 is found this, "Then the high priest rent his clothes, saying, He hath spoken blasphemy; what further need have we of witnesses? Behold, now you have heard His blasphemy." So, the second segment of blasphemy is a human claiming to be God! You have already seen several quotations concerning the papal claim of Divinity. You are very familiar with the claims of the church like this one from the Catholic Encyclopedia which says, "This judicial authority will even include the power to forgive sins."[12] So, there can be no honest question that the power here pinpointed in prophecy is the papacy! As to its persecutions, history clearly reveals it. But, so does the church.

The rector of the Catholic Institute of Paris, Henri Marie Alfred Baudrillart, referred to the attitude of the church toward persecution. He said, "When confronted with heresy, she does not content herself with persuasion, arguments of an intelluctual and moral order appear to her sufficient, and she has recourse to force, to corporal punishment, to torture. She creates tribunals like those of the inquisition, she calls the laws of the state to her aid, if necessary she encourages a crusade, or a religious war, and all her (horror of blood) practically culminates into urging the secular power to shed it, which proceeding is almost more odious . . . . for it is less frank . . . than shedding it herself." This was taken from "The Catholic Church, The Renaissance and Protestantism," pages 182 and 183.

The Today's English Version of the Bible says, "And it was given authority over every tribe, nation, language, and race."

The prophecy portrays the fact that this beast power comes to the place where it takes on the same basic psychology of the papacy, and becomes world-wide in advancing that papal psychology and teaching. As a matter of fact, the beast actually becomes a tool for the papacy. The beast grows to be so much like the old papacy that it is impossible to tell that it is not the papacy itself. Look at this, "And power was given him (by those supporting heads and horns) over all kindreds, and tongues, and nations."

Once again, let me remind you that it is very difficult to share these things with you and not give the impression of being critical. Please keep in mind that it is very difficult to reveal these things as well as discover them.

This prophecy reveals that this power, driven on by the Roman heirachy and other religious and civil leaders and organizations, becomes that anti-Christian power that brings the world to its life and death decision. This multi-faceted organization is the Anti-Christ. It becomes the one opposing force to God and His laws. Terrible as it sounds, it will be the one power that places you in a position of choice. And your choice will mean life eternal or eternal destruction. The prophecy says, "And all that dwell upon the earth shall worship him, whose names are not written in the book of life of the Lamb slain from the foundation of the world." (Revelation 13:8) And then it gives this little piece of advise, "If any man have an ear, let him hear." In other words, if you are truly spiritual at all, then pay attention.

This first beast of Revelation 13 is a power that is very much like the old papacy, the persecuting church. The beast has many, many civil and religious bodies making up its force and power. It will have the Catholic Church as its major contributor, but fallen Protestantism is right in there supporting it, too. All countries in the world will be aiding it. And the individual humans who are actively engaged in its last day assault will be those who are not born-again believers in Christ Jesus, and will be lost! As you go on into the remaining verses in this explosive thirteenth chapter of Revelation, you will see what brings people into the

127

beast power's organization, and the life-saving element that will keep some out.

Like a stone rolling down a steep mountain side, this prophecy gains momentum as it goes on. The worst is yet to come!

John the Revelator, now turns away his thought from the first beast and switches to another one. He says, "And I saw another beast coming up out of the earth; and he had two horns like a lamb, and he spake as a dragon." [vs. 11].

The second beast is seen coming up out of the earth. The first beast came up out of the sea. So, this other beast has some opposite beginnings. Revelation 17:15 defines the difference by telling us this, "The waters which thou sawest where the whore sitteth, are peoples, and multitudes, and nations and tongues." The second beast had to come up in a place just opposite that of lots of people and populated nations. So, it comes into being in a isolated area.

This second beast comes into being as the first beast was initially set back in its growth. So, the second beast was coming into its own when the first beast got its deadly wound. It was coming into being sometime around the late 1700's.

Another description of this second beast is that it has "two horns like a lamb." The other beasts in Bible prophecy all had crowns on their heads or horns. This, then, would be a nation without a king or a church without a pope! I told you that this prophecy would be almost unbelievable and now you are beginning to see why.

This second animal in Revelation 13 is a country that formed its Declaration of Independence in 1776! It is a country that was "discovered" and not "conquered" like all others before it. It is a country that was a barren, almost desolate land before becoming a great world-wide power! Sure, it is our own beloved United States of America!

The second animal is portrayed as a "lamb" when all the other ones were being pictured as fierce and wild. God

128

could not have used a better animal than a gentle lamb to portray the peaceful, early nation of ours, could He?

The "two horns" correctly portray the two basics of our Constitution, Civil and Religious Liberty. This is amazing! The United States of America is directly spoken of in the Bible!

It might be well to make something clear right here. I was born in America. I served in our armed forces. I salute the American flag, sing the Star Spangled Banner, and love my country. But, by all means, I love the Lord, too. Like Jesus said, "Give to Caesar what is Caesar's and give to God what is God's," I support my country and my God. So, when God's Word says something so important about my country as to put it in a unique and critical prophecy, I want to know what it is all about. If God is warning me that my country is going to do something in the future, I want to know what it is. You feel the same way. So please, remember that this is all coming from God's Word, and being written about by someone who loves his country, his church, "baseball, apple pie, and Chevrolets," and all that!

Look at what this prophecy says about our country: "And he exerciseth all the power of the first beast before him, and causeth the earth and them which dwell therein to worship the first beast, whose deadly wound was healed. And he doeth great wonders, so that he maketh fire come down from heaven on the earth in the sight of men, and deceiveth them that dwell on the earth by the means of those miracles which he had power to do in the sight of the beast; saying to them that dwell on the earth, that they should make an image to the beast which had the wound by a sword, and did live. And he had power to give life unto the image of the beast that the image of the beast should both speak, and cause that as many as would not worship the image of the beast should be killed. And he causeth all, both small and great, rich and poor, free and bond, to receive a mark in their right hand, or in their foreheads; and that no man might buy or sell, save he that had the mark, or the name of the beast, or the number of his name." [vss. 12–17].

That is almost beyond human comprehension! How in the world is the United States of America going to do something like that? Even though it seems utterly impossible, God's Word says it will most definitely be fulfilled. Can you imagine that?

It says that the U. S. will say: "to them that dwell on the earth that they should make an image to the beast, which had the wound by the sword, and did live." Many parts of the country have different accents, but most of them have this one phrase: "He's the spitting image of his dad." It is used to illustrate how a young boy looks so much like his dad. Now, if a boy is the "image" of his dad, is he the same person as his dad? No, they just look alike, act alike, and have the same basic principles. So, this text tells that the United States, the country that was founded on religious liberty, the separation of the church from the state, will adopt the same principles of religious persecution as the papacy once had in the Dark Ages!

The first time I heard this, I got pains in my stomach. Man, it was all tied in knots! You may feel the same way right now, but, would you not prefer discovering these facts for your eternal welfare, even if your stomach did start turning somersaults? The next facts are not going to help relieve the tension, but look at them anyway.

The Bible says that our beloved country would cause "all, both small and great, rich and poor, free and bond, to receive a mark in their foreheads; and that no man might buy or sell, save he that had the mark, or the name of the beast, or the number of his name."

You probably have heard people, through the years, talk about "The Mark of the Beast." Well, this is where they got that term. That "mark" of the beast, or its name, or the number of its name will determine whether or not you will be able to buy or sell.

It is all going to boil down to your obeying the laws of the land or the laws of your Lord! If you are faithful and true to the Lord, refusing to go along with these laws, then you will find yourself, for a short time before Christ returns, without a job, without any visible means of support, without the right to work and earn a living, without the right to carry on a normal life, and eventually, be under the death penalty. Through the union of all these spiritually fallen religious organizations and worldly governments into that beast power in the first part of Revelation 13, a law will be passed. It will also be passed in these very own United States of America.

Our country is going to become so corrupt, so full of rotten and warped politics, so off balance because of economical, political, and spiritual disorder and discord, that laws will be passed making it mandatory to have the mark of the beast in order to earn a living or buy the bare necessities of life. The law of the land will say, "Have the mark of the beast and you will live!"

God says, in Revelation 14:9-10, this, "If any man worship the beast and his image, and receive his mark in his forehead, or in his hand, the same shall drink of the wine of the wrath of God, which is poured out without mixture into the cup of His indignation; and he shall be tormented with fire and brimstone in the presence of the holy angels, and in the presence of the Lamb."

It is a matter of life or death! So, if you are going to be punished by God and lose eternal life if you receive the mark of the beast, then you have got to find out what the mark is, and make sure that you do not get it.

Okay then, what is the "mark of the beast?" Since that beast will be almost identical to the Roman Catholic Church in its early Dark Ages life, then it is only fair to ask, what is the mark of the church? They will be almost identical. So, if you discover the mark of the Roman Catholic Church you will have the same mark.

What is a "mark" anyway? Some people will tell you that a "mark of a man" is his clothes. Others say that a "mark of a homebuilder" is the quality of his work and the style he uses. But, with a king, or a nation, or a church, the mark is its authority or principles.

One of the most popular and great leaders of the American Division of the Roman Catholic Church was Cardinal Gibbons. He wrote a book dealing with the church's principles and doctrines entitled "Faith of Our Fathers." On page 14, he said this, "Of course the Catholic Church claims that the change of the Sabbath from Saturday to Sunday was her act. And this act is a (notice this now) mark of her ecclesiastical authority." In the same paragraph, he makes it well known that there is no basis for this change in the Holy Scriptures, by saying, "You may read the Bible from Genesis to Revelation and you will not find one single line authorizing the sanctification of Sunday. The Scriptures enforce the religious observance of Saturday, a day which we never sanctify."

But, notice that the "mark" of the Roman Catholic Church is the act of changing God's Holy Sabbath Day to the Day of the Sun!

The thing that will bring together these religious leaders into the common union under this "beast" power will be the complete agreement, and usage, of Sunday instead of the Biblical seventh-day Sabbath, Saturday! There will be a common bond between fallen Protestantism and Catholicism, the Sunday! That day, and its observance, is to become a world-wide issue. The majority will want to follow the custom and tradition of Sunday. The issue will mount. Other climatic things such as economics and energy will escalate it. Oil, coal, and energy products will become unbelievably costly. Crops will fail to produce the food necessary to feed the world. Wars and strife will be erupting all over the face of the globe. Crime will reach an all time high, far exceeding the wildest imagination. Jobs will become super-scarce. Inflation will skyrocket to the place where the bare necessities will be so expensive that only a few will be able to afford them.

Diseases will be rampant. It will be, as the words of the

Bible itself described it: "A time of trouble such as never was since there was a nation."

It will be at this time that Lucifer will make his move! With the greatest intensity he has ever mustered up for any conflict against the Creator, he will send his host of fallen and powerful angels to ingeniously impress unsuspecting minds across the globe with the idea that all these terrible and traumatic troubles are coming to planet earth because man has departed from God.

A revival to turn man back to God will sweep across the world. Men, women and young people come under the delusion of those persuasive angels, who, the Apostle Paul says, will be "transforming themselves into the apostles of Christ." In II Corinthians 11:14, Paul adds, "And no marvel (or wonder)! For Satan himself is transformed into an angel of light." Through the many religious leaders within that beast power will come the great appeal to return to the proper keeping of "God's Holy Day," and they will mean, not the true Sabbath day, but the traditional day of the sun, the first day of the week, Sunday.

The great push will be on. Churches will see overflowing crowds into their sanctuaries on the Sun-day. Ministers of all faiths will be begging the world to "remove the wrath of God from off our shores. Return to a day of rest. Return to keeping the Lord's day. Make Sunday that true worship day God intended it to be." The majority will fall hook, line, and sinker for it all!

The majority will accept the false revival, and still the "wrath of God," as they call the troublous times, will not be removed! Things will get only worse and worse.

Jesus put it like this, "And men's hearts shall fail, for looking after the things coming upon the earth." The havoc increases its intensity! Satan makes another magnanimous move! Once again his demonic angels sweep into action. Once again they begin to make deep impressions and inspirations in the minds of men. They will suggest to these duped world leaders that the wrath will not be lifted until everyone follows the law! As this satanic solution is suddenly seized upon by religious leaders, too, the cry goes out to make every man, woman, and child obey the law. This is where the ''image to the beast'' will come in. Whether or not our own country makes the first one, it is not certain, but it will be in a place of real world influence. Then the United States will make that predicted law of laws.

At the present time, on the statute books of every single state in the union, there is a law called ''The Blue Law.'' These ''Blue Laws'' already state that it is a violation to do business on Sunday. They all carry a penalty for breaking these laws, But, believe it or not, your Bible is predicting that the whole nation will adopt a Sunday law!

The law that makes it mandatory to worship God on Sunday, and forbidding work on that day, will become an act of Congress. Our own President of the United States, thinking that he will lead our nation and the rest of the world out of all its Herculean hardships and handicaps, will actually send the bill to Congress himself!

Shortly afterwards, every other nation will follow suit. Does this sound utterly impossible? Listen, it is already in progress! A few years ago the President of the Lord's Day Alliance was on nation wide television. By the way, when they speak of ''the Lord's Day'' they are speaking of Sunday, not the Biblical Sabbath. This sincere man said this, ''We aim to put Sunday worship on the same basis exactly as the seventh-day Sabbath was in the days of the children of Israel.'' Someone, obviously shocked by this statement, spoke up and said something to the effect that back in the days of Israel's keeping the Sabbath the Israelites were a theocracy, a people under the direct leadership of God, and not a democracy, a people under the leadership of people. They reminded the speaker that under certain circumstances in those old days that when a man broke the Sabbath he was put to death. Then that person asked the guest this question, ''Do you mean that you want to go that far . . . if a person doesn't keep Sunday, he'll be put to death?" That religious leader said, "That's exactly what I mean. That's what we're working for!"

When man reaches the depths of spiritual decay and passes that law, it will not only be that "image" our country is to make to the old ancient papal principle of persecution, it will set up the procedure for man receiving the "mark of the beast."

You see, any law forbidding something must have a penalty, a punishment, for all violators. The punishment has already been spelled out for you in the Holy Word of God. It says that "as many as would not worship the image of the beast should be killed." The death penalty will be issued for all dissenters!

Identification cards, stamps, booklets, or direct engraving of a special mark to allow the followers of the law of the land to buy and sell, and carry on their activities, will probably come to pass. The Bible does not specifically say what it will be. But, the ones who follow the false day of tradition, taking their stand with the majority in direct opposition to the known Word of God, will have these temporary "benefits." Those who love the Lord more than life and possessions will not, of course, be extended these privileges.

. They will be worked with by the authorities. The clergymen, rejecting the Bible and its God-given principles, will no doubt be called upon to counsel with these "heretics." When all manner of persuasion has failed, and these people steadfastly follow Christ's commands and are "faithful unto death," then they will be placed under conviction and be sentenced to die.

To make an example of all the "heretics" a universal day of destruction will be set by all the world's leaders. Faithful, Christ-loving men, women, and young people, from all walks of life, will be placed in jails awaiting their death. It will seem as if all heaven has rejected them. They appear to have no Savior. Ridiculed, rejected by friends and loved ones, and all alone, they are looked upon as the "poor fools who have brought all this trouble on us."

As the final minutes tick away before the death decree is carried out, all hope seems to be lost. Just seconds before the appointed time there will come "a great voice out of the temple of heaven, from the throne, saying, It is done!" The eastern sky will become a blazing light of beauty, and Christ's words in Matthew 24:30, rejected by many through the years, will become a glorious reality, "Immediately after the tribulation of those days shall the sun be darkened, and the moon shall not give her light, and the stars shall fall from heaven, and the powers of the heavens shall be shaken; and then shall appear the sign of the Son of man in heaven: And then shall all the tribes of the earth mourn, and they shall see the Son of man coming in the clouds of heaven with power and great glory."

All through the Bible, from Genesis practically through to Revelation, a crucial picture is portrayed. It is the great controversy between Satan and God, Jesus Christ, the Holy Spirit, and His church! Lucifer's one goal in his soon-to-end life has been, and will be until that end, to crush Christ, Christianity, and the truth! Very, very soon he will have his most successful attempt. Even though it will be temporary and short, millions upon millions will fall for his fantastic fraud. Those who follow him in this swindle of all swindles will be destroyed, with him, in the lake of fire.

Those who earnestly pray to God for guidance, study diligently these things through the Bible, and follow all of the revealed truth they have, will receive eternal life with Christ Jesus. Those who are true to Him in the end, will be those who have learned these facts and will not fall for this world-wide hoax. They will discover the truth about His holy day and observe it in obedience and out of loving gratitude.

There will be only two groups. Which one will you be in?

9/COUNTER-ATTACK

"A Spectacular Simultaneous Strategy"—that is the only way I can describe it in a few words. Maybe you can conceive of a better way to explain it. Sweeping across Christendom is a sensational occurrence. It seems as if it suddenly started simultaneously in practically every denomination with Christianity. Men, women and young people from all walks of life and with all types of social and financial background are experiencing the same thing. It is a mysterious moving among some special members in churches all across our land. Honest-of-heart laymen are beginning to sense something. Spiritual questions are now crying out in their hearts and minds for true Biblical answers. Words and sentences are almost leaping off the pages, making indelible impressions. Sincere believers are sensing inconsistencies. A spirit of discontent is beginning to permeate the pews. Scriptural misapplication no longer sails over their heads. Even the youngest Christians feel an invisible inspiration to make sure that what they are being taught is truly one hundred percent Biblical. Great truths, long hidden in the dust of the centuries of traditional teachings, are now being discovered. There is a "Spectacular Simultaneous Strategy" behind it all.

Through the centuries Satan has successfully sold his pagan, anti-Christian teachings of sun worship to unsuspecting spiritual leaders within Christianity through one ingenious method. That has been through a slow, deliberate, and imperceptible chipping away at the Biblical foundation of Christendom.

A very obese man was asked how it was that he had gotten so amazingly overweight. He honestly replied, "Ounce by ounce." By the same token, Christianity has become so intricately invaded by pagan sun worship, inch by inch. Satan's scheme did not occur over night. It was a slow, gradual, creeping injection of innovations. Minute changes, so undetectable, were ever so quietly introduced. Little by little, ever so small particles of the God given principles of Christianity were diluted by the counterfeit. Year after year, decade after decade, generation after generation, and century after century more and more emphasis was being placed on sun worship and less and less on Christianity. You know the rest of the story.

But, back to that "Spectacular Simultaneous Strategy." In a much overlooked prophecy in the book of Revelation you will find the strategy that is not only spectacular but being carried out simultaneously with Satan's last ditch stand! In Revelation 14:6–12, you will discover what several million people affectionately refer to as "The Three Angels' Message." It is the portrayal of three angels commissioned to carry certain critical communiques from the Creator to His earthly creatures. The apostle John saw and heard them. He recounts it this way: "And I saw another angel fly in the midst of heaven, having the everlasting gospel to preach unto them that dwell on the earth, and to every nation, and kindred, and tongue and people, saying with a loud voice, Fear God, and give glory to Him; for the hour of His judgment is come; and worship Him that made heaven, and earth, and the sea, and the fountains of waters. And there followed another angel, saying, Babylon is fallen, is fallen, that great city, because she made all nations drink of the wine of the wrath of her fornication. And the third angel followed them, saying with a loud voice, if any man worship the beast and his image, and receive his mark in his forehead, or in his hand, the same shall drink of the wine of the wrath of God, which is

138

poured out without mixture into the cup of His indignation; and he shall be tormented with fire and brimstone in the presence of the holy angels, and in the presence of the Lamb. And the smoke of their torment ascendeth up for ever and ever; and they have no rest, day nor night, who worship the beast and his image, and whosoever receiveth the mark of his name. Here is the patience of the saints, here are they that keep the commandments of God, and the faith of Jesus.''

Notice that this prophecy deals with three "angels." Maybe you have already discovered this truth, but I really had never grasped the tremendous significance of it before. I had always read this passage and mentally pictured three white robed, winged supernatural beings somewhere up in the sky almost shouting out admonitions for people to turn to God.

Here is where I was way off base. In Bible prophecy an "angel" represents one of two things. Either it means a "message" or "a messenger." By not realizing this, I had missed that whole valuable point! The passage, itself, actually tells which one it is. It says that the angel had "the everlasting gospel" to preach to the world. Every week, across the globe, the gospel is supposed to be preached to everyone who will listen. Who does that preaching of the gospel? Sure, "ministers" do it! All right, then, are these men of the cloth behind their pulpits angelic or human? Naturally, you know that they are very definitely human. So then, this prophecy is portraying a special message that is to go to every person on earth. It is picturing a "message" and not a "messenger."

Okay, what is that special message? The passage said that the first angel had "the everlasting gospel" to give to the world. It did not say, "a fresh, new gospel," or "an ultra-modern gospel," or even "a remodeled gospel." It is the "everlasting one!" So, then this special, world-wide message is actually a divine plea for mankind to come back to a true, non-mythical, non-superstituous, non-sunworshipping, one hundred percent Biblical gospel.

The first angel also had another definite divine desire in his message. He said, "And worship Him that made heaven, and earth, and the sea, and the fountain of waters."

Since you know now that it was Jesus Christ our Lord who actually made the earth and everything in it, you can also see that this is just one more heaven-sent appeal to you to get back to the keeping of the only memorial God gave you of His Son's creation. The seventh-day Sabbath is the only divinely ordained method of paying homage to Christ's creation of your world in six days.

Do you see what is happening? At the same time Satan is making his greatest assault against Christ and Christianity, God is not sitting back, idle and helpless. He had dictated that definite data be dispatched to dying humanity for it to devour before the deadline. When the second angel said that "Babylon is fallen . . . because she made all nations drink of the wine of the wrath of her fornication," he was actually describing a divine educational program.

You see, "Babylon" has always been portrayed in the Bible as the direct opposition of truth. Since pagan sun worship was conceived in Babylon, it has always represented the direct opposite of Christianity. In Revelation it is a symbol of that one great fallen religious body who, in the end of time, vigorously promotes the counterfeit religion you have been reading about.

Therefore, this second angel is symbolically portraying how God will expose this great counterfeit religious teaching to the sincere and dedicated believers within Christendom. It is this exposure, this divine educational program, that I named "A Spectacular Simultaneous Strategy." At the same time Satan is seeing his most successful swindle being carried out, our loving God is moving, through His Spirit, among the church members in every single congregation, large or small, in the city and the country, and bringing these long lost truths to their attention. Every single day sincere seekers are sensing His sweet Spirit speaking to them of His sacred Sabbath as well as scores

140

of other scriptural subjects He seeks for them to understand and accept.

This very book may be the one method the Lord has chosen for you to find out these fantastic facts! Through special sacrifices of several million sincere believers who have, themselves, come to this great discovery, this "Three Angels' Message" is going to all the world in many different ways. Through the radio, television, printed page, and personal endeavors, God is carrying on that spiritual educational work for humanity. All the time this thrilling story has been right there in Revelation, and the majority never, ever are made aware of it!

There is an additional segment to this last-day message besides the spiritual educational endeavor. The third angel portrayed its solemn message. It is the warning that those who adopt these anti-Christian teachings, in the place of the known word of God, will loose eternal life.

Henri Frederic Amiel, the French philosopher, once demanded, "Truth above all, even when it upsets and overwhelms us."

As you read [in the last chapter] of the way in which Satan plans to bring about the final act in his swindle of all swindles, you might have gotten a little upset. The prospect of a law being passed in your own beloved country, whereby you will be told to compromise your standards and Biblical beliefs to accept the popular, widely accepted substitute day under the penalty of death, might have easily overwhelmed you. It did me. It does almost every sincere person who learns of it for the first time. But, more and more you can see the eternal principles involved in it all. Very soon every man, woman, and young person will have to make that eternal decision. It now becomes perfectly clear that it is more than simply going to church on one day or another. It is a choice between God and the country. It is accepting and following the laws of God or the laws of the land. Now you can begin to grasp the true importance of that passage in Revelation 18:4, where the Lord cries out to all His loving believers and followers the plea,

"Come out of her, My people, that you be not partakers of her sins, and that ye receive not of her plagues." Now you can see so clearly that it is one of God's last calls for the born-again believers to come out of these churches in which these anti-Christian, counterfeit, sun-worshipping principles and teachings have crept. It is a call for you to separate yourself from every organization, regardless of how friendly and kind its members may be, that are not following all his teachings to the letter.

Now you are able to correctly understand who the prostitute, the vile woman, of Revelation 17 is. You know now that it is speaking of this great body of fallen Christianity when it describes her as a "great whore that sitteth upon many waters; with whom the kings (leaders) of the earth have committed fornication, and the inhabitants of the earth have been made drunk with the wine of her fornication."

Sure, you can discern now that this is speaking of all these fallen religious groups who have caused its followers to accept Satan's counterfeit teachings.

Now you can figure out that it is the great conglomeration of fallen religions teaching these mixtures of Christianity and sun worship that the Bible describes in Revelation 17 as an impure woman who has on her head "a name written, Mystery, Babylon the great, the mother of harlots and abominations of the earth." God is educating you through these odd prophecies. He is also protecting them from being wiped out by putting them across to you in strange terms, and then saying to you, "Search the Scriptures, wherein you think you have eternal life," and "Study to show thyself approved unto God, a workman that needeth not to be ashamed, rightly dividing the word of truth." Yes, God is simultaneously bringing an understanding of these long neglected truths in prophecy to the world. Just think, you are a part of fulfilled prophecy as you read.

Is not this fantastic? Just think, as you read your Bible now great new meanings are in store for you. Familiar passages will now explode in exciting and special meaning for you. You will start to see clearly why Jesus said many things like, "But in vain they do worship me, teaching for doctrines the commandments of men." Now you can understand fully why near the very end of the great account of future events, the book of Revelation, these words are found, "Blessed are they that do His commandments, that they may have right to the tree of life, and may enter through the gates into the city." Our relationship with Christ will be based on a true love for, and willing obedience to, all His teachings.

In this prophecy of the special messages God sends to us in these last days the very last words were these: "Here is the patience of the saints, here are they that keep the commandments of God, and the faith of Jesus." The word "patience" comes from a Greek word that means "endurance." So, after the three angels' message pleads with man to return to a complete and true obedience of God's commands, it states that the "endurance" of the saints, the true children of God, will be marked off in direct contrast to those who will be lost. The one thing that will mark them off will be their keeping His holy day, the seventh-day Sabbath, and faithfully witnessing to others about their soon-coming Saviour.

A very talented minister of the gospel has given many fine books to the Christian world. In the front of one book he gives his permission for others to use any part of his messages if they will further the cause of Christianity. I want to take him up on that offer and relate a beautiful story to you. In it he tells of a minister who was trying to relax by taking a leisurely horseback ride. The minister let loose of the reins and allowed the horse to wander wherever he wanted to go and at his own pace. I often thought about this story and wondered if the minister did this because he, himself, had been led around by so many others. Nevertheless, the horse led him through the woods into a clearing. At the end of the clearing there was a small humble home. As the horse slowly walked over to the home the man saw a woman sitting on the porch. He asked the woman if she lived there. She replied, "Yes, sir, just Jesus and me, just Jesus and me."

The minister stated that there was such a peace about that place and the woman that was beyond words.

One day soon these spectacular and stunning prophecies are going to be fulfilled. There will come that church-state legislation. The vast majority will go along with the laws of the land, and of course, eventually receive the mark of the beast. According to the most dependable work in all creation, the Bible, this majority will loose eternal life. In comparison, only a small few will remain faithful to the Lord and His Holy Word. These will receive the greatest of all gifts—life eternal with Him. They will love the Lord so much that if it boiled down to only one person, each one would be willing to say, " 'Just Jesus and me.' If no one else will be faithful, it will not keep me from following Him all the way. I'm going to remain true. I'm going to make it because He will walk with me, support me, and give me courage and strength to stand firm for the truth. It's going to be just Jesus and me."

10/CALCULATED CATASTROPHE

William Shakespeare wrote: "There is a line by us unseen that crosses every path, the hidden boundary between God's patience and His wrath." If anyone ever has any question about the longsuffering and patience of God, then the mere fact that He has allowed this great battle of Satan to continue nearly six thousand years now should quiet it once and for all.

The Lord has allowed these centuries of war, strife, crime, broken homes, false religions, crooked politics, and sickness to continue for one reason. That is, to allow man time enough to reason it all out in his mind, understand the overall plan of salvation, and come back to that right relationship with his Creator.

Many people have wondered when Jesus will finally come and bring all this chaos to an end. The Apostle Peter wrote that the Lord will keep His promises, but there is a reason for His delay in coming. In Second Peter 3:9 he said, "The Lord is not slack concerning His promise, as some men count slackness, but is longsuffering to us-ward, not willing that any should perish, but that all should come to repentance." The long delay in winding up all the affairs of this life is out of love and concern for mankind.

There will come a definite prophesied time when that unseen line will be crossed, and God's wrath will have to finally be unleashed on rebellious planet earth. That unleashing of God's wrath is known as the seven last plagues.

Many writers have described this catastrophic event in many varied and lewd ways. Since I had discovered that many of the traditional teachings had been altered through the invasion of sun worship, I determined to see exactly what the Bible did teach about these awesome plagues. A very sound and studious seminary professor was willing to take the time away from a very hectic schedule and candidly answer a long list of questions that puzzled me. This gifted teacher had also, many years before, come to an understanding of the basic Bible beliefs as originally given to Christianity. I valued his judgment. As a result of that interview, I was able to piece together a sensible and Biblical concept of the seven last plagues.

First, I discovered that these devastating unnatural disturbances will come after the Sunday closing law has been passed throughout the world and continue right up until the designated time for the decree against all objectors is to be carried out. You will see this is so very distinctly stated in this tremendous prophecy. They will not occur until right after the world has fallen so low as to make its God-defying decree.

In the seventh chapter of Revelation you will find that the Lord takes specific precautions to insure that the first plague does not begin until after the Sunday closing law has been established world wide. In verses 1–3, you find the precaution stated this way, "And after these things I saw four angels standing on the four corners of the earth, holding the four winds of the earth, that the wind should not blow on the earth, nor on the sea, nor on any tree."

You are very familiar with the word "news." My dictionary states that it is, "Fresh information concerning something recently taking place." The word, as you know, came from the Biblical terminology of the "four winds" and the "four corners of the earth." In other words, North, East, West, and South. The Bible uses the terms just to indicate that all directions are to be taken into consideration. The Bible does not recognize a flat earth with four corners.

So, here in this first verse is the symbolic picture of four angels hovering over the earth holding back these ever-ready plagues, preventing them from striking earth prematurely.

The prophecy goes on, "And I saw another angel ascending from the east, having the seal of the living God; and he cried with a loud voice to the four angels, to whom it was given to hurt the earth and the sea, saying, Hurt not the earth, neither the sea, nor the trees, till we have sealed the servants of our God in their foreheads."

This picture of the Lord extending His patience to the world one last time before He unleashes His wrath is typical of His love. But, did you notice that the Lord first seals His people before He pours out one year of terrible plagues on sinful, rebellious earth? Right now, I can imagine the thought racing through your mind, "One year of plagues? How did he determine that?"

In the eighteenth chapter of Revelation the writer is speaking of that apostate religious organization that, with full world leader cooperation and support, initiates that Sunday closing law. The results of her sinful, anti-Biblical act is, she is doomed. In verse 8, it reads, "Therefore shall her plagues come in one day, death, and mourning, and famine; and she shall be utterly burned with fire; for strong is the Lord God who judgeth her."

Since it has already been established that a "day" in Bible prophecy equals one literal year, then the Bible is telling you that when man becomes so spiritually low as to pass this great satanically inspired law, there will fall on this earth one year of the most horrifying, agonizing, catastrophe humans will ever witness.

So then, look carefully at the seven last plagues of the Bible. The entire sixteenth chapter of Revelation is devoted to them. Beginning with the very first verse we read this, "And I heard a great voice out of the temple saying to the seven angels, Go your ways, and pour out the vials (bowls) of the wrath of God upon the earth."

At this climactic time of earth's history, everything will

be completely out of balance. Jesus said in Matthew 24:21, "For there shall be great tribulation (affliction and pressure in the original Greek), such as was not since the beginning of the world to this time, no, nor ever shall be."

News, the fresh information concerning everything chaotic taking place, terrifies the average person. It will be exactly like Jesus said in Luke 21:26, as recorded in the New English Bible, "Men will faint with terror at the thought of all that is coming upon the world." The problems confronting the world are unbelievable. World leaders are being assassinated and replaced in ever-growing numbers. Riots rock large cities. Travel is almost impossible because of the enormous expense of gasoline and oil. Those who, somehow, do make vital trips are subjected to hijacking and open robbery. The stupendous inflationary cost of groceries, coupled with the gigantic city, county, state and federal taxes, make it almost impossible for families to have anything more than near starvation meals. Women must be accompanied by two or three men to be halfway safe on any street. Diseases and infections are known by almost everyone. State hospitals are grossly overcrowded. Tensions and tempers are high. No one knows what is going to happen next. Life is filled with anxiety. Death is even a relief for many.

Then it happens! The evening television news breaks with the shocking story of an unusual epidemic breaking out in various parts of the world. Reporters give the gruesome picture from scores of cities in many different countries around the world. It seems as if no country, large or small, is exempt from the throes of ulcerated boils! In Revelation 16:2 it says, "And the first went, and poured out his vial upon the earth, and there fell a noisome (foul-smelling) and grievous (painful) sore upon the men which had the mark of the beast, and upon them which worshipped his image."

Crippled transportation and over-worked physicians make it nearly impossible for medical teams to be sent to these afflicted areas. As more and more reports come in, it is

148

now determined that the epidemic is almost world-wide. Doctors' waiting rooms are crowded with pushing, demanding, crying, and agonizing victims. Drug stores' and discount houses' pharmaceutical sections are jam packed with sufferers seeking some kind of salve or solution that will relieve the stinging, burning, itching anguish.

Medical science is stymied! No analgesic or anesthetic is effective. Nothing seems to be able to desensitize the throbbing malaise. The number of afflicted increases daily. Almost every man, woman, and child is tormented by this never-before-equaled epidemic. A few isolated cases are discovered where entire families have not been affected. Every one of these cases, it seems, is in families and individuals who do not have the government's special identification mark.

As man begins to sense that something supernatural is going on, the news gives another alarming announcement. Something very unique and weird is taking place along the seashores of the world. Verse 3 describes it this way, "And the second angel poured out his vial upon the sea, and it became as the blood of a dead man; and every living soul (being) died in the sea."

You are familiar with the term "coagulated blood." That is blood that changes from its normal liquid state into a clot or jelly mass. Did you notice that when the second angel poured out his bowl into the sea, "It became as (or like) the blood of a dead man"? Can you imagine that? Men, women, and children flock to the seashore to see the awesome spectacle of all forms of sea life that lie lifeless on the shores. The eery sight of stiff large and small fish, long twisted eels, broken-opened clams and oysters, and an occasional now-harmless shark or barracuda is only made worse by the uncanny still and burgundy-colored sea. No waves beating rhythmically on the shores. Just a ghostly calmness. It is not long before the stench of dead life penetrates the inner areas beyond the shoreline. The anxiety increases as men begin to sense a definite supernatural aura overshadowing these events.

149

Imagine the deafening dismay when the earth experiences the addition of the third plague to the already stunned population. In verse 4, it says, "And the third angel poured out his vial upon the rivers and fountains of waters, and they became blood." Notice that they did not become "as the blood of a dead man," or coagulated, but "became blood." Can you grasp the horror of walking to the kitchen sink, reaching over to turn on a faucet for a drink of water, and out comes real, pulsating blood? Every lake and river is changed from its life giving liquid to the shocking flow of real blood! The lagoon, pond, dam, spring, reservoir, ditch, brook, puddle, creek, and cistern is now a plentitude of that red plasma!

The Bible makes it clear that this is actual blood in the two verses that follow this stupendous third angel's plague. In verses 5 and 6, you read this account of the blood being definite punishment for a specific sinful crime. It says, "And I heard the angel of the waters say, Thou art righteous, O Lord, which art, and wast, and shalt be, because thou hast judged thus. For they have shed the blood of saints and prophets, and thou hast given them blood to drink; for they are worthy."

This punishment of the third plague is a rebuke against two things. First, the world piled up a horrible account against itself for actually taking the lives of men ordained of God as prophets and spokesmen. And, second, the plague was falling on those who had already decreed to take additional lives of "saints," precious born-again believers who remained faithful to God and His law. The Bible was treating their death decree as if their blood had already been shed.

Sometime later, during the year, something else so supernatural that men could not possibly deny its origin and would curse the Creator for it, starts to take place. The ozone layer, the narrow layer in the stratosphere about 20 miles above and around us that weakens the force of the ultraviolet-like rays of the sun as they strike the earth, slowly begins to diminish! As it does, look at what the

Bible says, "And the fourth angel poured out his vial upon the sun; and power was given unto him to scorch men with fire. And men were scorched with great heat, and blasphemed the name of God, which hath power over these plagues; and they repented not to give Him glory."

I had the privilege once of inspecting some roofs of buildings at the Atomic Energy Plant in South Carolina. As an inspector and I walked across a very long and large building, I commented on the fact that that particular roof was constructed of reinforced concrete many, many feet thick. I asked the polite inspector, "What in the world would we need such a thick reinforced concrete roof for?" He reminded me what was going on beneath the roof. As I realized the awesome force men were experimenting with beneath me, I wasted no time in viewing the area and made a hasty exit down off the building.

According to the Holy Scriptures, great structures will not be able to shield man from the intense heat of the fourth plague. Gigantic generators will break down under the overload as men turn to air conditioners and fans to relieve the searing rays of the sun. The thermometer escalates! The temperature becomes unbearable! The simmering and seething sun intensifies!

This passage states that "men were scorched with great heat." I wondered if the original Greek, in which this was written, really was "scorched." You see, my dictionary told me that the word means "a superficial burn, a mark caused by heat, as a slight burn." That seemed like a really awful infliction. But, the original word "scorch" used here was "kaumatizo." That means "to parch, or wither with heat." I guess that is why the New English Bible says that men were "fearfully burned" during the fourth plague.

Then, the direct opposite occurs! In verses ten and eleven is found this, "And the fifth angel poured out his vial upon the seat of the beast; and his kingdom was full of darkness; and they gnawed their tongues for pain, and

151

blasphemed the God of heaven because of their pains and their sores, and repented not of their deeds."

Since this great anti-Christian organization portrayed as the "beast" has now, at this time, gotten practically all the world under its control and influence, and the largest majority have gotten the mark of the beast, you can easily understand this passage. It is simply a symbolic way of stating that the entire earth becomes enveloped in complete darkness.

Since this is the direct opposite of the burning sensation of the merciless sun, the darkness would bring deep and penetrating cold. As anyone with a sunburn knows the sickening effect of coming into an air-conditioned room for any period of time, this passage brings out the anguish and aching effect the plunging temperature has. The deep, penetrating cold on already badly burned bodies is excruciating! Once again, wicked men shake their fists towards heaven and curse God!

These first five plagues cover almost that entire twelve months' period. Wicked humanity, that has rejected the God of heaven and His loving laws, has become an insane society. Driven on by wicked angels, they take out their vengeance and wrath on that small number who "are the cause of all our troubles." They decide that now they have to rid them from the face of the earth. False religious leaders, under the same satanic inspiration, urge the extermination of these "trouble making rebels who have brought these afflictions upon mankind," and will demand the death decree be carried out.

In a very unusual and odd manner, the prophecy describes Satan's final act in world-wide hoax. In verses 12–16 are found these terms, "And the sixth angel poured out his vial upon the great river Euphrates; and the water thereof was dried up, that the way of the kings of the east might be prepared. And I saw three unclean spirits like frogs come out of the mouth of the dragon, and out of the mouth of the beast, and out of the mouth of the false prophet. For they are the spirits of devils, working miracles, which go forth unto the kings of the earth, and of the whole world, to gather them to the battle of that great day of God Almighty."

Right in the middle of all this, the Lord Himself injects this word of warning to you as you read all this. In verse 15, He says, "Behold, I come as a thief. Blessed is he that watcheth, and keepeth his garments, lest he walk naked and they see his shame." In other words, the Lord reminds you, as you are reading these traumatic events, that He is definitely going to come in the middle of it all, and warns you to be ready with the robe of His righteousness. Now, back to the plague before you.

"And he gathered them together into a place called in the Hebrew tongue Armageddon." This complicated prophecy started off by talking about the angel pouring his vial out into the great Euphrates River. It dried up the river so "that the way of the kings of the east might be prepared." In order to understand this, you will have to look at a few other passages in the Bible. They may seem unrelated at first, but as they are all put together the amazing picture will come together like a jigsaw puzzle.

Way back in the Old Testament book of Numbers you have the story of the Israelites starting off from Mount Sinai to go to the Promised Land. To keep order and unity, each of the tribes, the large families, were assigned a definite place to pitch their tents. In chapter 2, and verses 1–3 is this account, "And the Lord spake unto Moses and unto Aaron, saying, Every man of the children of Israel shall pitch by his own standard, with the ensign of their father's house; far off about the tabernacle of the congregation shall they pitch. And on the east side toward the rising of the sun shall they of the standard of the camp of Judah pitch throughout their armies . . ." Can you recall what was the standard, the ensign, the emblem or trademark, of the tribe of Judah? It was the lion. Keep that emblem in mind as you read a statement about Jesus in a prophecy in Revelation 5:5. It says, "And one of the elders said unto me, Weep not, for the Lion of the tribe of Judah, the Root of David, hath prevailed to open the book . . ." Jesus was referred to, here, as the "Lion of the tribe of Judah."

Confused? Well, look at what you read earlier in Revelation 7:2 about the four angels holding back the winds of strife. It says, "And I saw another angel ascending from the east, having the seal of the living God . . ."

The tribe of Judah pitched their tents on the east side.

Jesus is referred to as "the Lion of the tribe of Judah."

The angel who sealed the true Christians before the plagues fell came from the east. It appears as if the orders for all activities on earth come from the east.

Ezekiel 43:1–2, look carefully at the first part of his description of things he saw in the vision, "And he (the angel) brought me to the gate, even the gate that looketh toward the east; and, behold, the glory of the God of Israel came from the way of the east; and His voice was like a noise of many waters, and the earth shined with His glory." Are you beginning to sense the meaning of all this?

Jesus gathered his twelve disciples together and told them quite a lot about His second coming. Look again at those familiar words, and see if you might have overlooked something. In Matthew 24:27, Jesus said: "For as the lightning cometh out of the east, and shineth even unto the west, so shall also the coming of the Son of man be."

This sixth segment of the seven last plagues is actually telling you about a fact very few ever realize. The "kings of the east" represent God the Father, Jesus Christ the Son, and The Holy Spirit, as well as all of heaven's host!

Revelation chapter 21 talks about the new heaven and the earth that will be established. It states that the headquarters of God will one day, after the new earth has been established, move on to that new, regenerated planet earth. In the first three verses it reads, "And I saw a new heaven and a new earth; for the first heaven and the first earth were passed away; and there was no more sea. And I John saw the holy city, the new Jerusalem, coming down from God out of heaven, prepared as a bride adorned for her husband. And I heard a great voice out of heaven saying, Behold, the tabernacle (the dwelling place) of God is with men, and He will dwell with them, and they shall be His people, and God himself will be with them, and be their God.''

Just to make absolutely sure no one misunderstands this tremendous revelation, verse 22 states catagorically that God the Father and Christ the Son are both there together, ''And I saw no temple therein; for the Lord God Almighty and the Lamb are the temple of it.''

The sixth angel symbolically opens up the way for all Divinity to come! The way that is prepared is seen in the unusual terms, ''And I saw three unclean spirits like frogs come out of the mouth of the dragon, and out of the mouth of the beast, and out of the mouth of the false prophet. For they are the spirits of devils, working miracles, which go forth unto the kings of the earth, and of the whole world to gather them together to the battle of the great day of God Almighty.'' Here is a picture of that multi-faceted, fallen religious organization as it makes its final persuasive plea for all nations to enforce that Sunday law death decree. By the satanically-inspired persuasion and cooperation, this Anti-Christ brings about the end of things. ''And he (the Anti-Christ) gathered them together (the whole fallen world) into a place called in the Hebrew tongue, Armageddon.'' The word Armageddon is derived from two words, ''Har,'' which means ''place,'' and ''megedon,'' which means ''a cutting to pieces, or slaughter.'' So, then, when this great anti-Christian force reaches the place where it causes the leaders of the world (''the kings of the earth'') to jointly decree that on a certain specific designated day all those who do not have the special indentification mark, and who refuse to obey the world-wide Sunday law, will be put to death, it actually brings the world to the place of its own slaughter.

This is so dramatically seen by the events that immediately happen in the seventh plague, ''And the seventh angel poured out his vial into the air; and there came a great voice out of the temple of heaven, from the throne (God's voice), saying, "It is done!" [verse 17].

The attempt to carry out the death decree is the final act in Satan's attempted scheme of all schemes! When the faithful, born-again lovers of Christ are doomed to destruction, Divinity steps in! The world-wide hoax meets its prophesied destiny! Look at what the Bible says about it, "And there were voices, and thunders, and lightnings; and there was a great earthquake, such as was not since men were upon the earth, so mighty an earthquake and so great. And the great city was divided into three parts, and the cities of the nations fell; and great Babylon came in remembrance before God, to give unto her the cup of the wine of the fierceness of His wrath. And every island fled away, and the mountains were not found. And there fell upon men a great hail out of heaven, every stone about the weight of a talent; and men blasphemed God because of the plague of the hail, for the plague thereof was exceeding great." Even as their destruction falls on them, wicked and fallen mankind curse God!

It is quite interesting to discover something about this hail that falls at the end that wipes out wicked mankind as well as buildings and homes. It is said that the weight of the stones was about that of a talent. A "talent" consists of 3,000 shekels. One shekel is a little over .021 pounds. So, 3,000 shekels would weight 63½ pounds! No wonder the earth is practically beaten to a pulp.

After the seven last plagues, another terrifying event takes place. In Revelation 19:17–18 this unnerving occurrence is told, "And I saw an angel standing in the sun; and he cried with a loud voice, saying to all the fowls that fly in the midst of heaven (this time it is the atmosphere), Come and gather yourselves together unto the supper of the great God: that ye may eat the flesh of kings . . . the flesh of mighty men, and the flesh of horses . . . the flesh of all men, both free and bond, both small and great."

Can you imagine that? The vultures are called in to clean up the destruction of the seven last plagues. Man,

156

you just cannot afford to have this happen to you, much less miss out on the great eternal life Jesus has provided for you through His death on the cross of Calvary! You have just got to give Him all of your heart, and follow all His teachings.

Remember Revelation 7:3 where the four angels were told not to start the seven last plagues until "we have sealed the servants of God in their foreheads." Well, the Bible tells you that there will be two identifying marks, or seals, placed on all of mankind. One is the mark of the beast, placed on fallen wicked and God-rejecting humanity. The other is the seal of God placed on those who really love Him and keep all His commandments.

You know now what that mark of the beast is, but what about the "seal" of God? A little Scripture search and you will discover a rich and rewarding lesson.

Way back in the time of the weak and gullible Persian King Ahasuerus, we find a story involving a Hebrew gatekeeper, Mordecai, who raised his uncle's daughter, Esther. Over 465 years before the birth of Christ, the book of Esther tells the whole story of an intrigue that could have destroyed the whole Jewish nation. Esther became the queen. She and Mordecai fasted and prayed for Divine guidance before Esther went to the king personally to foil the plot. The Lord honored their prayers, the king saw through it all, and the Jews were saved. In the eighth chapter of Esther you will find the king granting Mordecai permission to send out an official letter to all the world about it all. In verse 10 is recorded these words, "And he wrote in the king Ahasuerus' name, and sealed it with the king's ring, and sent letters by posts on horseback. . . ."

What was it that gave the letter power and authority? It was the official seal of the king. Mordecai no doubt dropped some wax onto the paper, and pressed the king's ring into the hot wax. The impression of the king's ring in the wax gave it the official authority of the king.

Every nation has its own seal of authority. Did you ever hear this little poem:

Scotland has it's thistle,
England has it's rose,
Everybody knows
where the shamrock grows;
France has it's lilly
blooming on the hill,
But the great American emblem
Is the one dollar bill.

Now, of course, you recognize that is not really the great American emblem or seal. You have seen it many times. Every time the President of the United States speaks on television, he is usually seen behind a desk or rostrum that has the great seal draped over it.

Did you know that the Bible tells you what the great seal of your Heavenly Father is? A few passages and you will see. First, Jeremiah 10:10-12. Here the difference between the true God, the Lord, and false gods is made distinct, "But the Lord is the true God, He is the living God, and an everlasting king; at his wrath (the seven last plagues) the earth shall tremble, and all nations shall not be able to abide His indignation. Thus shall ye say unto them, The gods that have not made the heavens and the earth, even they shall perish from the earth, and from under these heavens. He hath made the earth by His power, He hath established the world by His wisdom, and hath stretched out the world by His discretion."

The difference between the true God and false gods of the world is clearly seen in the Lord's power to create the heavens and the earth! Couple that thought with something found in Jeremiah 51:15-16. Speaking of the Lord, Jeremiah says, "He hath made the earth by His power, He hath established the world by His wisdom, and hath stretched out the heaven by His understanding. When he uttereth His voice, there is a multitude of waters in the heavens; and He causeth the vapours to ascend from the ends of the earth; He maketh lightnings with rain, and bringeth forth the wind out of His treasure.''

So, the Lord's authority is based on His creatorship. Therefore, the seal of God must be the sign of God as Creator!

This sign really becomes significant when you think about a modern seal so familiar to us all. Sometime or another, you have had to engage the services of a Notary Public. That Notary's seal made the document official. Your signature was witnessed and substantiated as true by that Notary.

Now think about this. A Notary's seal is composed of three parts. First, the Notary's name. Second, his title. Third, his designated territory. The seal would have these three segments on it, and read something like this, ''Thomas A. Jones, Notary Public, Jackson County, Maine.'' Name, title, and territory.

The seal of God, His sign, would bear the same three parts, have the same three segments. Did you know that?

Do you also know that the Bible gives you that seal, the sign of God, with the three vital segments contained therein? You will find one very vivid example of it, in all places, right in the middle of His own revealed law. That is right! Right in the middle of the Ten Commandments God gave you his His own seal, His own sign!

In Exodus 20:8–11 you find this, ''Remember the Sabbath day to keep it holy. Six days shalt thou labour and do all thy work. But the seventh day is the Sabbath of the Lord thy God; in it thou shalt not do any work, thou, nor thy son, nor thy daughter, nor thy manservant, nor thy maidservant, nor thy cattle, nor thy stranger that is within thy gates. For in six days the Lord (name) made (title— Creator) heaven and earth (territory), the sea, and all that in them is, and rested the seventh-day; wherefore the Lord blessed the Sabbath day, and hallowed it.''

That is tremendous! No wonder Satan has been working these nearly 6,000 years to hide the truth of the sacred Sabbath day from mankind. The Sabbath is God's sign!

Once you come to the realization of the sacredness of the seventh day Sabbath, and determine in your heart to lovingly and willingly keep that day holy as He intended for you to do, the Sabbath becomes two beautiful things to you.

First, it is a sign of yours. It is a sign to the world that despite all the modern teaching of evolution, you believe in a special creation by the Lord in six literal days. It is your sign to the world that you accept the validity of the Bible's account of creation week. It is your living witness, your sign, to all His creations that you believe in Him, the Creator.

This first sign made a dramatic change in one atheist I know. I was conducting a special lecture series in a university city when I met this avowed disbeliever in the Bible, God, and Christ Jesus. Prior to the opening night I had been asked to visit this man by his stepmother. She told me that he was a near genius and that it was very difficult for her to try to witness to him about Jesus because he talked so far above her. Every conversation with this young man of 25 was a real put-down for her.

So, somewhat hesitantly, I visited the young postgraduate student. I had just barely introduced myself when he began a long, long lecture on evolution. When I use the term "long, long lecture," that is exactly what I mean. Several hours passed before I was able to get in a word. Finally, sensing that there was nothing I could say to this really vocal atheist, I stood up, looked for a long deliberate time at my watch and said, "I'm sorry, but I am going to have to leave. My watch indicates that it is nearly four o'clock." He started to stand when I said, "By the way, did you ever hear about my watch?"

He replied that he had not, and I said, "Well, would you believe it if I told you that several months ago I came home late one evening to find that one of my children had left a light on in the garage near my workbench. When I went into the garage to turn off the light I slipped on a roller skate. As I started to fall I desperately reached out

160

for something, and I grabbed the workbench. As I was falling I pulled the workbench over. There was a loud bang as nails, wires, tools, screws, nuts, bolts and all kinds of jars and bottles went flying across the garage floor. Would you believe it, when I started to pick up all those things I found that all those screws, nuts, bolts, springs, and glass had fallen together to make this watch!"

The young man looked right into my eyes and said, "Bull!"

I looked right back into his eyes and replied, "Yes, that's my sentiment exactly for your theory of evolution," and walked out.

You can imagine my shock, when on the opening night of this evangelistic crusade, I looked across the audience to see, sitting right there on the back row, as far away as he could be and still be in the audience, this young man.

Night after night he attended the four-week meeting. I lectured on these things you have been reading, and many others, appealing to the audience to accept the God-given, non-mythical, non-sunworshipping, Biblical way of life, keeping all His commandments.

One night I gave a call for men and women to give their hearts and lives to Christ the Creator of heaven and earth, and re-Creator of life through His death on the cross. You will never know the joy that came to the entire audience when that former atheist came forward in tears to make a new life in Christ.

Afterwards I asked him what had caused him to come to a Christian crusade. He told me, "Your watch!"

Then he went on to tell how silly that story I had told him was, and as he thought about it, how absurd the theory of evolution was. As he attended college classes and would hear the bell ring at the end and beginning of each class, the clock was a constant reminder. He stated that there was no more logic in the world coming together by accident than my watch. As he decided to just listen to the lectures, something happened to him. The truth became clear. He had had great difficulty in accepting the traditional

Christian teachings when they had been so invaded by pagan sun worship. The things you have been reading made him determine that true Christianity, minus all the non-Biblical fantasies, was for him! He started keeping the true seventh-day Sabbath, the Lord's day. The Sabbath was a sign for him. It is for you.

Second, the Sabbath is not only a sign that you believe in the Creator, Christ Jesus, and His word, it is also a sign that you are in the process of true sanctification through Christ. Sanctification is the setting apart of a life for Christ. Believe it or not, that is exactly what the Lord has promised to do when you give Him your whole heart and life and start keeping all His commandments. Now in case you might feel like this seems somewhat fanatical, please look at Ezekiel 20:12. It records the Lord's words like this, "Moreover also I gave them my Sabbaths, to be a sign between me and them, that they might know that I am the Lord that sanctify them."

As you begin to lovingly and appreciatively live for the Lord and keep His holy day He will begin that sealing process that will set you apart in safety from those who receive the mark of the beast. As in the days of Israel's departure from ancient Egypt, when the Lord poured out the plagues on Egypt, and protected His people completely from it all, God will do that for you very soon as He unleashes His seven last plagues. He will give you special protection and preservation.

In the ninth chapter of Ezekiel we have a perfect example of how the seal of God will be your protection during those terrible plagues. In verses 4-6, we read this, "And the Lord said unto him (His angel), Go through the midst of the city, through the midst of Jerusalem, and set a mark upon the foreheads of the men that sigh and that cry for all the abominations that be done in the midst thereof. And to the others He said in mine hearing, Go ye after him through the city, and smite; let not your eyes spare, neither have ye pity. Slay utterly old and young, both maids, and little children, and women, but, come not near any man upon whom is the mark; and begin at my sanctuary. Then they began at the ancient men that were before the house.''

It made a real difference that night if a person had the mark, the seal of God, or not. One day soon, it will make all the difference in this world and eternity, whether or not you have God's seal. With that seal, you will pass unharmed through the seven last plagues and on into the new eternal life with Christ.

By the way, that is not my idle claim. The Lord put that down in writing. In Psalm 91:7–11, the Lord's written guarantee goes like this, ''A thousand shall fall at thy side, and ten thousand at thy right hand; but it shall not come nigh thee. Only with thine eyes shall thou behold and see the reward of the wicked. Because thou hast made the Lord, which is my refuge, even the Most High thy habitation, there shall no evil befall thee, (now get this) Neither shall any plague come nigh thy dwelling. For He shall give His angels charge over thee, to keep thee in all thy ways.''

Lunken Airport in Cincinnati, Ohio was the scene of a most unusual and amazing display of courage and trust. Richard Vonderhaar flew a single engine Cessna airplane and landed it all by himself. Amazing? Yes, when you consider that Richard was blind. Richard took off, flew, and landed as perfectly as anyone with good vision. He did it all by explicitly obeying the verbal commands of his instructor. Everyone said it was beautiful!

You have a beautiful, yet challenging, experience before you. You have learned of Satan's swindle of all swindles. His world-wide hoax has successfully defrauded millions from having a beautiful and sane, sensible and scriptural relationship with their Creator, Jesus Christ. Scores and scores of sincere Christians are missing out on heaven's richest blessings through the counterfeit, watered-down, sun worship-Christian mixture so prevalent today. Maybe you are one of those who really loves the Lord and has been sincerely ignorant of these great truths. A new life

163

awaits you. A higher, closer walk with Jesus may be yours.

The Lord says to you, in John 14:23, "If a man love me, he will keep my words; and my Father will love him, and we will come unto him, and make our abode with him."

It is my deep belief that there is no way for you to read about the wholesale departure from Biblical teachings and not be affected . It is also my sincere opinion that you would not have gone this far in this book if you did not have that deep and inner desire to truly keep Christ's words. Aristotle said, "All men naturally desire knowledge." The honest person wants knowledge far more than a simple acquiring of facts. And if you have come this far in your reading this very different book, you have got more than a surface interest. Therefore, you will be thrilled to know the answers to all these religious questions plaguing minds today.

I have stated in this book that there are about eighteen basic segments making the sum total of Christian doctrine. Space will not allow complete coverage of all these vital segments in one reasonably sized paperback book. Therefore we have divided this documented story of the world-wide hoax into two books. "All In The Name Of The Lord, Book Two" contains the remainder of those doctrines invaded by pagan sunworship. Modern Christendom has almost no concept of the original Christian doctrine. Most demoninations in existence in this age of advanced technology are actually teaching that blend of sun worship and Christianity with all sincerity and earnestness, never aware of these gross errors.

I would like to share the truth with you concerning these invasions. You will be stunned at the ingenious ways in which the enemy of your life has successfully swindled humans through their acceptance of these sun worship theories and practices as actual Christián teachings. You will be shocked at how far we have actually departed from the simple Bible truth. You may have to also examine some of your own concepts once again. But, I believe you demand to know the truth and will welcome this opportunity to delve into a deeper study of this world-wide hoax. In "All In The Name Of The Lord, Book Two" you will be given the Biblical portrayal of what actually takes place just before, during and after the stunning second coming of Jesus.

In addition, you will see the explosive Biblical explanation of whether or not Jesus will actually return in your lifetime.

You will discover why there are so many different denominations in existence today teaching so many different doctrines.

Also you will learn the spectacular ways the Lord employed through the years to insure that His teachings would prevail in spite of the overwhelming odds against it.

A special section answers the age-old question of what constitutes "the unpardonable sin." You will be able to determine with certainty if a person has committed the sin for which there is no pardon.

In this easy-to-read second book you will be able to determine for yourself if there is any organization in existence today that is following all the teachings of Christ Jesus. You can learn of the requirements necessary for a group of people to actually make up the remnant church. And by the way, the dedicated followers of the Lord who could meet those requirements will not be made up of people who go to a church simply because it is on the corner near home, because mom and dad were members, or because it is popular. This unique portion of this second book will be a real help in your desire to walk as He did.

One unique chapter that tells of the most unusual circumstances surrounding Elvis Presley, Bing Crosby, and Guy Lombardo (who all died within a period of 50 days) may prove to be one of the most challenging concepts you have ever considered.

"All In The Name Of The Lord, Book Two" is not

available in bookstores. If you would like to receive your own personal copy of this explosive book please fill in the order form found on the opposite page. When your request for what may prove to be the most valuable information you have ever discovered is received, we will rush a copy directly to you.

An even greater adventure than the one you just completed in this first book awaits you in this unique second book. You owe it to yourself to investigate the intriguing and inspirational facts found in "All In The Name Of The Lord, Book Two." A rich reward is guaranteed!

May heaven help you in your determination that what you do in the future may truly be "all in the name of the Lord."

Concerned Publications, Box 1024, Clermont, Florida 32711

Please send me "All in the Name of the Lord, Book Two." I am enclosing $2.00 plus 50¢ for postage and handling = $2.50

Name _____
Address _____
City _____ State _____ Zip _____
Send check or money order—no cash or C.O.D.'s please.

REFERENCES

1. GOOD NEWS FOR MODERN MAN. Scripture text is from THE GOOD NEWS BIBLE-Old Testament: Copyright (c) American Bible Society 1976; New Testament: Copyright (c) American Bible Society 1966, 1971, 1976. Used by permission.

2. THE NEW ENGLISH BIBLE. Copyright (c) The delegates of the Oxford University Press and the Syndics of the Cambridge University Press. 1961, 1970. Used by permission.

3. THE NEW TESTAMENT IN THE LANGUAGE OF TODAY By William F. Beck. Concordia Publishing House (c) 1963. Used by permission.

4. THE WEYMOUTH'S TRANSLATION OF THE NEW TESTAMENT By Richard Francis Weymouth. Copyright Harper and Row Publishers, Inc. Used by permission.

5. THE CHRISTIAN BAPTIST By Alexander Campbell. Copyright Gospel Advocate Company. Used by permission.

6. FAITH OF OUR FATHERS by James Gibbons. Copyright Our Sunday Visitor, inc. Used by permission.

7. LETTERS TO YOUNG CHURCHES by J.B. Phillips. Copyright, 1947, 1948, by MacMillian Publishing Co., Inc. renewed 1975, 1976 by J.B. Phillips. Used by permission.

8. CONVERT'S CATECHISM OF CATHOLIC DOCTRINE by Peter Geirmann. Copyright 1930, B. Herder Book Co., St. Louis.

9. CANON AND TRADITION by Heinrick Julius Holtzman (Ludwigsburg: Druck and Verlag Von Ferd. Riehm, 1859) P. 263 German.

10. FAITH OF MILLIONS. Used by permission of Our Sunday Visitor, Inc. Copyright by John A. O'brien, 1963, 1974.

11. CATECHISM OF THE COUNCIL OF TRENT FOR PARISH PRIESTS. Copyright 1934 By Joseph F. Wagner, Inc. New York.

12. CATHOLIC ENCYCLOPEDIA. Copyright St. Joesph's Seminary and College. Used by permission, Vice General, Archdiocese of New York.

13. THE LIVING BIBLE. Copyright 1971 by Tyndale House Publishing, Wheaton, Illinois. Used by permission.

BIBLIOGRAPHY

ANCIENT CITIES AND TEMPLES-BABYLON, Albert Champdor.

ANCIENT PAGAN SYMBOLS, Elizabeth Goldsmith.

ANTIQUITIES OF THE JEWS, Flavius Josephus.

BABYLON AND NINEVAH, A. H. Layard.

BABYLONIAN AND ASSYRIAN RELIGION, Samuel Henry Hooke.

BIBLE MYTHS, T. W. Doane.

BRYANT'S ANCIENT MYTHOLOGY, Jacob Bryant.

CAMBRIDGE ANCIENT HISTORY-EGYPT AND BABYLONIA, J. B. Bury.

CATHOLIC ENCYCLOPEDIA, THE.

CHRISTIAN WORSHIP: ITS ORIGIN AND EVOLUTION, Louis M.O. Duchesne.

CURIOUSITIES OF POPULAR CUSTOMS, William S. Walsh.

DECLINE OF THE MIDEVIL CHURCH, THE, Alexander C. Flick.

DEVELOPMENT OF THE CHRISTIAN RELIGION, THE, Cardinal Newman.

DICTIONARY OF SYMBOLS, THE, A. J. E. Cirlot.

ENCYCLOPEDIA AMERICANA, THE.

ENCYCLOPEDIA BRITANNICA, THE.

ENCYCLOPEDIA OF RELIGIONS, THE, J. G. FURLONG.

FAITH OF OUR FATHERS, James Gibbons.

FAUSSETT'S BIBLE ENCYCLOPEDIA, A. R. Fausset.

HALLEY'S BIBLE HANDBOOK, Henry H. Halley.

HISTORY OF THE DECLINE AND FALL OF THE ROMAN EMPIRE, Edward Gibbon.

HISTORY OF THE CHURCH, THE, Philip Schaff.

HISTORY OF ROME, THE, Theodor Mommsen.

JEWISH ENCYCLOPEDIA, THE.

MAN AND HIS GODS, Homer W. Smith.

NEW CHAFF-HERZOG ENCYCLOPEDIA-RELIGIOUS KNOWLEDGE, S. M. Jackson.

NINEVAH AND ITS REMAINS, Austin Henry Layard.

OUTLINE OF HISTORY, THE, H. G. Wells.

STANDARD DICTIONARY OF THE ENGLISH LANGUAGE, THE.

STORY OF THE WORLD'S WORSHIP, F. S. Dobbins.

TWO BABYLONS, THE, Alexander Hislop.

YOUNG'S ANALYTICAL CONCORDANCE TO THE BIBLE, Robert Young.